WANTED – ONE BODY!

WANTED – ONE BODY!

by Charles Dyer

JOSEF WEINBERGER PLAYS

LONDON

WANTED – ONE BODY!
First published in 1961
by Josef Weinberger Ltd
12-14 Mortimer Street, London, W1T 3JJ
(pka English Theatre Guild Ltd)

Copyright © 1961 by Charles Dyer

Reprinted 1964, 1966, 1968, 1975, 1983

Revised edition © 1990 by Charles Dyer
Reprinted 2002

ISBN 0 85676 040 4

WANTED – ONE BODY! was presented by Rita Theatres Limited at the Oxford Playhouse and on tour with the following cast:

MISS BARRACLOUGH	Elizabeth Gott
MABEL BIDDY	Fiona Thompson
ANNE BEALE	Maryann Turner
TED JOHNSON	John Payne
MR BLUNDELL	J Grant Anderson
MR MICKLEBY	Charles Dyer
AGNES	Ann Hunter
DR BROWN	Eric Hillyard
MR SORRELL	John Cross

Directed by Charles Dyer

WANTED – ONE BODY! was subsequently staged at the Whitehall Theatre, London and televised for the BBC with the following cast:

MISS BARRACLOUGH	Joan Sanderson
MABEL BIDDY	Dora Bryan
ANNE BEALE	Elspet Gray
TED JOHNSON	Peter Mercier
MR BLUNDELL	Leo Franklyn
MR MICKLEBY	Brian Rix
AGNES	Edna Morris
DR BROWN	Larry Noble
MR SORRELL	Gerald Cross

Directed by Charles Dyer

CASTING NOTE

The BARRACLOUGH SISTERS were designed for one actress but a splendid effect is obtained when two actresses achieve similarity in make-up, hair styles and mannerisms. Each must be equally powerful. The sisters are domineering women: the more fearsome they are, the greater the thrills and comedy.

The roles of BLUNDELL and MICKLEBY are written as uncle and nephew, but are as effective when played by two mature or two young men: in which case, the term "Uncle" can be cut. Whatever the age group, MICKLEBY remains respectful to his superior.

*** *** ***

APPRECIATIONS FROM THE PRESS

"I can never resist farce and laughed helplessly." – *Daily Mail*

"Of all the television farces from the Whitehall this was the most successful." – *Daily Mirror*

"The laughs came loud and often." – *Daily Telegraph*

Somewhere in England is Greenacres, home of the late Mr Barraclough. The play is set in the Lounge during a winter's afternoon and night, many years ago.

ACT ONE

ACT TWO

Opening Music

ACT ONE
Scene One

TIME: Any time, but probably in the Twenties, when parlour maids bobbed, and undertakers wore black top hats. A dismal afternoon in the lounge at Greenacres with its mysterious panels, ornate pillars and creaking stairs, dusty books, drapes and shadows.

When the curtain rises, the room is in darkness, a few beams of watery light catching the sombre figure of FAITH *seated in the armchair* RC.

A stately woman of good height, greying hair, FAITH *is dressed entirely in black, and is shrouded in a veil. The hard lines about her mouth show no trace of sadness ... only bitter triumph.*

Lightning Flashes. Thunder Roars.

    (MABEL enters down the stairs. She is the perky maid, currently wallowing in the tragedy of it all. She has a black outdoors coat over her uniform and is creeping everywhere in squeaky shoes. She coughs and waits.)

FAITH   *(raising her veil)* Well?

MABEL   I found your black gloves, Miss Faith.

FAITH   Here, on the table. And switch on the lights. I'm tired of the dark.

    (MABEL clicks a switch by the archway and on come the lights. She creeps to the table R, deposits the gloves, then creeps back to C.)

MABEL   Ahem, miss.

FAITH   Well?

MABEL   Can we open the kitchen curtains, Miss Faith?

FAITH   The curtains are drawn as a token of respect for the dead.

MABEL	Yes'm. Aren't you cold, sitting there, Miss Faith?
FAITH	Naturally.
MABEL	(*nods fearfully towards the study*) Aren't you frightened, as well?
FAITH	Why, pray?
MABEL	With the late Mr Barraclough lying in that Study. Rest his soul.
	(MABEL, *as throughout, bobs respectfully on 'Rest his soul'.*)
FAITH	Not in the least.
MABEL	I thought the funeral was at two-thirty, I did.
FAITH	The Undertaker has been delayed by floods, and apparently his wife is expecting a baby.
MABEL	Fancy! You never think of undertakers having babies. 'Suppose it sort of restores their confidence in life.
	(*Outside a dog howls* MABEL *shivers, then creeps towards the hallway.*)
FAITH	(*shouts*) Mabel!
MABEL	Agh! (*Jumps.*) What?
FAITH	Stop creeping.
MABEL	I was doing it for the late Mr Barraclough. (*Pointing* R.) Rest his soul.
FAITH	Well stop. It's irritating and it's noisy.
MABEL	Yes'm.
	(*Thunder clap* MABEL *yelps.*)
FAITH	And pull yourself together. (*Rising angrily she moves to the desk.*)

MABEL	I'm afraid I'm a bit frightened, Miss, I'm afraid. It's the first time I've been in a house with a . . . a late person.
FAITH	It is merely the shell of a departed spirit.
	(FAITH *takes a stamped-addressed envelope from a little chest on the desk, and a letter from her bodice.*)
MABEL	But he was full of beans last week, Miss. Rest his soul. Now he's lying in there, just a poor empty shell.
FAITH	(*shouts*) Stop harping on his lying in the study. You're to post this letter in the village. After the funeral.
	(*In slamming down the chest lid,* FAITH *knocks an ornamental bell to the floor.*)
	Pick it up!
	(MABEL *creeps below her and returns the bell to the desk.*)
MABEL	I just wish I didn't have this crawling premonition, like a thousand feathers itching me stomach.
	(FAITH *licks the envelope flap and seals it.*)
FAITH	Here! (*Gives her the letter.*) And for heaven's sake stop moaning.
MABEL	(*creeping to* C) I'll try, Miss.
	(ANNE BEALE *enters* L, *a young woman in a black business-like two-piece costume. She carries a cup of tea.*)
FAITH	Mabel, don't creep!
	(MABEL *runs out* C.)
ANNE	It's five past three, Miss Barraclough.
FAITH	(*behind the armchair*) I have a watch of my own.

ANNE	A cup of tea for you. (*Puts it on the table.*)
FAITH	I didn't order tea, Miss Beale.
ANNE	Cook thought you might like one.
FAITH	I see. 'Cook thought'. It did seem strange for you to be so thoughtful.

(ANNE *moves towards the staircase.*)

Miss Beale! (*Pointing.*) There are no envelopes in my little chest.

ANNE	(*pausing on the stairs*) There are some in the study, I believe.
FAITH	Oh? (*Crosses above sofa, sipping her tea.*) Then be so kind as to bring them for me.
ANNE	If it's only one you need, I have some upstairs.
FAITH	(*without looking at her*) Kindly fetch my *own* envelopes. From the study. Or are you afraid of the ... 'late' person in there?

(*Lightning and thunder.* ANNE *crosses to the study door, where she hesitates.*)

Do you also share Mabel's simple notions of impending horror?

(ANNE *enters the study. The thunder roars.* MISS FAITH, *cup raised, runs her tongue over her lips. She frowns. Returning from the study,* ANNE *puts a bundle of envelopes in the little chest.*)

This tea is quite foul. Tastes bitter.

ANNE	You haven't achieved anything, asking me to go in there.
FAITH	You were my stepfather's secretary, and my stepfather is dead. Until such time as you leave, Miss Beale, you will make yourself generally useful about the house.

ANNE	(*to the stairs*) I shall do anything within reason.
FAITH	You will do anything without reason. (*To foot of stairs*.) And you know why.
ANNE	Honest explanations are wasted, I suppose?
FAITH	How right you are. Please let us not wrangle . . .
	(*Turning,* ANNE *hurries up the stairs.* FAITH *shouts the end of her sentence.*)
	. . . in the presence of the dead.
	(JOHNSON *has appeared in the hallway. He is in chauffeur's uniform, a rough diamond, personable yet terse and sinister.* FAITH *senses his presence. She moves* RC.)
FAITH	Well . . . (*Without looking at him.*) Johnson?
JOHNSON	No news, Miss Faith. The Undertaker's still waiting for his baby.
FAITH	This comes of dealing with a fool villager.
JOHNSON	Oh, it's the floods. His pallbearers can't reach the parlour, d'you see.
FAITH	And what about me? And the coffin in there?
JOHNSON	I suppose you'll both have to wait. (*He moves* L.)
FAITH	Just one moment! If you please.
	(JOHNSON *stops.* FAITH *places her cup and saucer on the table.*)
	I shall be dismissing all the servants after the funeral.
JOHNSON	Does that include Anne Beale?
FAITH	Of course. (*Turns her back.*) I had long decided to make a clean sweep when I became Mistress of Greenacres.

	(*She sets her hand against Caeser's bust and runs a finger down its profile.*)
JOHNSON	(*moving behind her*) You don't believe in wasting time.
FAITH	Nor in wasting anything.
JOHNSON	Because you've done someone a wrong.
FAITH	(*facing him*) Someone who?
JOHNSON	Anne Beale.
FAITH	Beale is a strange girl. A romancer. Heaven knows what she has told you.
JOHNSON	Everything. And I believe her.
FAITH	Such an ordinary little woman.
JOHNSON	I like her. We're going to be married.
FAITH	O-oh! (*Sits on the sofa, and looks him up and down.*) Well well well.
JOHNSON	(*to end of sofa*) Look, Miss, I'm after no trouble; but there's this Confession.
FAITH	Oh no no, I like having such a valuable document.
JOHNSON	(*angrily*) She's served your purpose. You've won.
FAITH	Shall we leave it that way?
JOHNSON	I want that paper you forced Anne to sign. Either give it me, or ...
FAITH	Or what? (*Flashing.*) You dare threaten me?
JOHNSON	Yes.
	(*They glare at one another, then* FAITH *smiles.*)
FAITH	(*purring*) You are hot-headed, Johnson. Vulgar. Insubordinate. But I admire you for it.
JOHNSON	I admire nothing about you.

FAITH	That's ... (*Curbs her anger*.) because you are immature, un-tutored. (*Huskily*.) And you could have silk against your skin.
JOHNSON	I can handle life. I know enough.
FAITH	You know absolutely nothing about handling me; yet you could, you know, so easily. I am rich now. My stepfather left a sizeable fortune. Naturally my sister must share this but I shall still be rich.
JOHNSON	So?
FAITH	So I shall need a personal secretary.
	(JOHNSON *moves impatiently towards the kitchen*.)
	Patience! Patience! Here is a way to regain your precious document.
	(JOHNSON *stops*. FAITH *rises, her back to him. She studies her hands*.)
	Oh yes. I need a man I could respect. A man worth training. Who'd learn grace and dignity – qualities which, frankly, you do not possess ... as yet.
JOHNSON	I'm happy.
FAITH	Because you are ignorant. Always other peoples' cars – never one of your own with a respected, well-paid position.
JOHNSON	My wife-to-be ... where does she figure in this stuff?
FAITH	Did you meet Beale here? At Greenacres?
JOHNSON	That's it.
FAITH	A few months. Hardly long enough to really know someone, especially a girl with an unfortunate background or has she not told you?
JOHNSON	She's told me about you.

FAITH	(*swings to face him*) Why not hear my side? No harm in waiting a while.
JOHNSON	Ha! (*Above sofa.*) So you could educate me.
FAITH	Yes! Say a trial period of three months.

JOHNSON		(*facing her*) Salary?
FAITH	*Very*	Double for a start.
JOHNSON	*fast*	And a car?
FAITH	*and*	We should probably have two.
JOHNSON	*crisply*	And the blackmail paper?
FAITH		Would be yours to destroy.

(FAITH *moves to him above the sofa.*)

	Or, if you preferred by then, we could post it to her.
JOHNSON	(*turns his back*) Hey, quite a proposition.
FAITH	I've waited a long time for this money ... Ted. Now it's mine, and I need someone to spend it on. (*Touching his arm, stroking it.*) Am I so *very* much older? I could be nice. And loving. (*She turns him round to face her.*) What have you to lose?
JOHNSON	My self-respect, d'you reckon? ... I could pity you, Miss Faith, if I didn't know how depraved you are.

(*Furiously she strikes at his face. He catches her hand, forcing her into a sitting position on the sofa's upstage side. She pants with temper and exertion.*)

	Oh no, Miss! (*Holding her wrist.*) Two can fight dirty. These old dark stairs. You can easily slip, fall out some window – there's always ways.
FAITH	(*hisses*) Get out. Out!
JOHNSON	For the time being. (*To doorway* L.) Shall you be needing the car for the funeral?
FAITH	I shan't need you.

JOHNSON	(*shrugs*) It's your funeral. (*Exits.*)
	(*Lightning flashes. Thunder roars. Rising,* FAITH *walks unsteadily to the archway. Weakly, she leans in sudden pain, clutching her throat and closing her eyes.*)
FAITH	(*shouts*) Mabel!
MABEL	(*immediately appearing*) Yes'm?
FAITH	You were listening. (*Furiously, drags her to* C.) Listening in the hall.
MABEL	Me, Miss? Ouch no, Miss. Not me, Miss. Never, Miss. No.
FAITH	(*to study doorway*) Remove that cup!
MABEL	Yes'm. (*Creeps to collect the cup.*)
	(*The front doorbell clangs dismally.*)
FAITH	Look in the hall. See who it is.
MABEL	Yes'm. (*Creeps to peer round the archway, creeps back.*) It's two gentlemen Miss. All in black.
FAITH	The Undertakers. About time. Show them in, and tell the other servants. Hurry! Hurry!
MABEL	(*creeps*) Yes'm.
FAITH	Don't creep!
	(MABEL *breaks into a run and exits with the cup and saucer.* FAITH *exits into the study, lowering her veil. Voices are heard off, then* MABEL *enters carrying two overcoats.*)
MABEL	(*moving to* LC) Would you wait in here, please.
	(MESSRS BLUNDELL *and* MICKLEBY *enter. The former is benign and scholarly. The latter is a jolly fellow with a briefcase. Each is dressed in dark jacket, striped trousers, black tie, and carries a bowler hat speckled with rain.*)

BLUNDELL   Thank you, m'dear, thank you. Sad weather,
                sad circumstances.

MICKLEBY   Your bridge is rumbling a bit. Almost under
                water back there.

MABEL   (*gloomily*) It floods every year – sort of
                bubbles under for winter.

MICKLEBY   Good gracious.

MABEL   The late Mr Barraclough's in his study.
                (*Bobs.*) Rest his soul.

                (*In unison,* BLUNDELL *and* MICKLEBY *hold their
                bowler hats across their chests.*)

BLUNDELL   ⎱
MICKLEBY   ⎰ (*bobbing together*) Rest his soul.

BLUNDELL   It must have been a tragic loss for your
                Mistress.

MABEL   Oh yes. Mind you, I shan't be sorry when
                he's sort of happily buried. Rest his soul. (*She
                bobs. So do the men.*) I've had the most
                awesome feeling of something lurking ever
                since he died.

MICKLEBY   L-lurking? (*Gives* BLUNDELL *a worried glance.*)

MABEL   Like eyes ... eyes ... watching ...
                watching ... all the time.

                (*Eyes wide,* MABEL *swings her finger slowly round
                the room and ends staring straight into*
                MICKLEBY'S *eye.*)

MICKLEBY   (*reacts*) Anybody's eyes in particular?

MABEL   No, sort of dis-embodied eyes, as though his
                spirit was having a last look round.

                (*A dog howls outside.* MICKLEBY *grabs*
                BLUNDELL'S *hand.* BLUNDELL *slaps him away.*)

BLUNDELL   Not to worry, m'dear. We are all given to, ah, imagination in sad moments. Ha ha.

MABEL   I suppose you gentlemen are used to horror —— being undertakers, I mean.

            (*A great bell cl-a-a-angs high above.*)

MICKLEBY   We're not undertakers.

BLUNDELL   No no, dear. We are solicitors.

MABEL   Oh streuth. But the Mistress thought . . . I mean . . . oh well, 'suppose it'll all sort itself out. 'Scuse me. (*She bobs and begins to creep out, then breaks into a run and exits* L.)

BLUNDELL   Peculiar girl.

            (BLUNDELL *hands* MICKLEBY *his bowler, takes the briefcase, then sits on the sofa.* MICKLEBY *puts their hats on the table* UR.)

MICKLEBY   I thought the funeral was at two-thirty.

BLUNDELL   Mm, it'll make us late at the office. Never-the-less, we must wait and read this Will. (*Sorting papers.*) Somewhat chilly in here.

MICKLEBY   (*at study door*) Not so chilly as old Barraclough in there.

            (*Lightning. Thunder.* MICKLEBY *hastens to beside the sofa.*)

BLUNDELL   I wonder if Miss Faith knows of the legacies? All this money to the domestic staff. That could add to the storm.

MICKLEBY   Uncle ——

BLUNDELL   Do not call me Uncle on business. Address me as Mr Blundell.

MICKLEBY   Yes sir, sorry. Uncle —— um Mr Blundell, d'you think she'll expect us to attend this funeral?

BLUNDELL   May have to, I daresay.

MICKLEBY   Oh Lord. (*Wanders* BC, *rubbing his hands.*) I can never enjoy funerals. Never think they're quite me somehow.

           (*Thunder.* MICKLEBY *swings round, his back to the bookcase* UL.)

           Bit of a spooky homestead. I'd hate to be here when midnight clangs.

           (*The great bell cl-a-a-angs. A panel slides open in the bookcase.*)

           Draughty, too.

           (*He rubs the back of his neck. Then slowly, suspiciously swings around – but the panel has closed. Now, he backs downstage to above the sofa, stooping to peer towards the study.*)

MICKLEBY   Mr Blundell, you don't think there *is* the odd watchful eye, do you?

           (BLUNDELL *finds himself gazing at the seat of* MICKLEBY'S *trousers.*)

BLUNDELL   Depends on your point of view. Here, better give this Will the once-over. Seems correct, but you've been handling the Account.

MICKLEBY   (*wandering* C) Oh, shouldn't worry.

BLUNDELL   (*document into briefcase*) I trust Madame is on good terms with her employees. (*He recites in a hollow voice.*)

           "Gold was the bait, And Hell was the price; So knock on my grave, Knock loudly, knock twice."

           (*The great bell cl-a-a-angs. Veiled* FAITH *enters from the study, gliding silently to beside* MICKLEBY.)

MICKLEBY   Knock on whose grave?

BLUNDELL   It's from the "Gold Digger's Death Knell".

MICKLEBY   Poor old Nell. (*Turning, he sees* FAITH *and screams.*) Aaaagh!

(BLUNDELL *rises, hurries over and, pulling him aside, slams the briefcase into* MICKLEBY'S *arms.* MICKLEBY *puts it on the chair against the panel.*)

BLUNDELL   (*apologetically*) Dear Madam, how do you do.

FAITH   You are late. Unforgiveable. (*Sweeps her gloves from the table, moves to the stairs.*) My stepfather is in the study.

BLUNDELL   Indeed yes. Our deepest condolences, Madam.

FAITH   You know the details. A quiet funeral. No flowers. No music.

(*The two men are at the first step, gazing up at* FAITH *on the staircase.*)

BLUNDELL   No flowers.

MICKLEBY   No music.

FAITH   We shall assemble in the hall. So move the coffin.

MICKLEBY   Oh, but Madam —— !

FAITHS   Move the coffin now! D'you hear? *Now.* (*Exits.*)

MICKLEBY   Uncle this is deadly.

BLUNDELL   Don't rub it in, boy.

(*Unhappily, they move to the study door.*)

MICKLEBY   She's mistaken us for the pallbearers. I won't do it. Why should we?

BLUNDELL   Because the lady hates being wrong. And we cannot afford to lose the Barraclough account. If Miss Faith requires the coffin in the hall, we must humour her.

MICKLEBY   Weird sense of humour.

(*The dog howls outside.*) BLUNDELL *pushes open
the door with a delicate finger. They are bathed in
weird green light.*)

BLUNDELL   Looks heavy.

MICKEBY   I think I'm going to cry.

BLUNDELL   There was a case once, I recall, of a fellow
who came-to just as they were lowering him
in.

MICKLEBY   What happened?

BLUNDELL   When he discovered where he was, he died
of shock. (*Braces himself and claps his hands.*)
Well!

MICKLEBY   (*backs away*) No! It's nobody's body I know
and I've no wish to meet it.

BLUNDELL   (*following him*) Mr Mickleby, what is the motto
of our Firm?

MICKLEBY   Labor Omin Vincit Sic.

BLUNDELL   Precisely.

MICKLEBY   And I feel very sick.

BLUNDELL   Courage, Mickleby, Courage. (*With a flourish.*)
Let us go!

(MICKLEBY *covers his eyes. Together they march
towards the study but, near the door,* BLUNDELL
sidesteps. MICKLEBY *marches in alone ... then*
BLUNDELL *follows.*)

(*Lighting and thunder. The dog howls.*)

(*The bookcase panel slides open. the arms of a
black-coated figure hover over the briefcase on the
chair. It extracts the will with one hand, whilst
returning another document with its other. The
bookcase slides closed.*)

(*A bang and yelp off.*)

MICKLEBY   Uncle, uncle! (*Hurries in.*)

BLUNDELL	(*appears* R) What is the matter, boy?
MICKLEBY	The l-lid. C-came open. There's an-n-n . . . arm sticking out.
BLUNDELL	(*peeps back*) Great heaven, so there is.
MICKLEBY	Is it moving?
BLUNDELL	Don't be silly. It's . . . just a dead arm, that's all.
MICKLEBY	Oh, you come across 'em every day?
BLUNDELL	All we need do is pop it back.
MICKLEBY	Thank you! (*Moves for his hat.*)
BLUNDELL	If Miss Faith discovers what we've done, she'll be furious.
MICKLEBY	No doubt.
BLUNDELL	Then pull yourself together. (*Authoritively.*) And pop that arm back!
MICKLEBY	If there's any popping, Uncle, you pop it.
BLUNDELL	Very well. Then stand guard. Poltroon!
	(BLUNDELL *marches into the study.* MICKLEBY *follows to stand guard, his back to the study door.*)
MICKLEBY	And hurry for pity's sake. Oh, this is one of those days.
	(*An arm appears, a bare shrivelled, veiny dead arm. It taps* MICKLEBY'S *shoulder.*)
	Yes, Uncle? . . . Aaaagh!
	(*He backs to* LC, *quaking. The arm advances, held by smiling* BLUNDELL. MICKLEBY *droops – arms on the sofa, head down.*)
BLUNDELL	Touché! (*He gooses* MICKLEBY.)
MICKLEBY	Uncle, how could you. (*Sits.*) I nearly died.

BLUNDELL   You will be pleased to learn, Hubert, there is
            nothing more gruesome in that coffin than a
            load of sand.

MICKLEBY   Where's the rest of him?

BLUNDELL   Where's all of him? (*Reads printing on the
            arm.*) "Wellington Window Dressing
            Company". Wonder where his boots went?

MICKLEBY   No!

BLUNDELL   Yes. Two of these and a sandbag under that
            shroud. Had you not been such a clumsy
            pallbearer, it might have gone undetected.

MICKLEBY   (*takes it*) You've got to hand it to me!
            (*Scratches his back.*) Comes in handy.

BLUNDELL   (*sits beside* MICKLEBY) Peculiar business, eh?

MICKLEBY   (*chin cupped in the hand*) Tell me more.

BLUNDELL   Do you recall the Case of the Crown versus
            Lapwing?

MICKLEBY   No.

BLUNDELL   Stupid of me to ask. Lapwing faked his own
            funeral and collected a fortune on his
            insurance.

MICKLEBY   But why should old Mr Barraclough want
            money? He was rich.

BLUNDELL   Too many girlfriends, perhaps.

MICKLEBY   What, at ninety? That's not wild oats, it's
            shredded wheat.

BLUNDELL   Hmmm. (*Grabs the arm.*) Hand it over. (*He
            takes it into the study.*)

MICKLEBY   (*follows to the door* R) Putting it back? Mr
            Blundell, I am not —— repeat not hanging
            around whilst you window-dress that missing
            link.

BLUNDELL	(*returns to* LC) Mr Mickleby, we shall play along with this awhile.
MICKLEBY	(*hoarsely whispering*) How can we read the Last Will and Testament of dummy arms and a bag o' sand?
BLUNDELL	Tantalising prospect, dear boy. I am curious.
MICKLEBY	I'm off. (*Collects his bowler.*)
BLUNDELL	Where are you going?
MICKLEBY	I've been called to the bar.
BLUNDELL	Mickleby! There is a coffin in there 'To Let'.
MICKLEBY	Yes; and I refuse to be the new tenant.
BLUNDELL	Mr Mickleby! (*Joining him.*)
MICKLEBY	No. Definitely, completely, inexorably no! I'm taking my bowler hat and my yellow streak and I am heading straight for town. And if I have to swim every inch, I shall be laughing all the way. (*He slams on* BLUNDELL'S *bowler in error.*) Good Luck! Oh. (*Lighting and thunder* FAITH *appears on the stairs, followed by* ANNE.)
FAITH	Now what is the delay? (MICKLEBY *replaces the hat on the table.* FAITH *descends.*)
BLUNDELL	I fear there's ah, slight case of mistaken identity, Madam. We represent Blundell, Blundell and Mickleby, Solicitors.
MICKLEBY	I'm Mickleby. He's the other two. (FAITH *stares at them angrily, incredulously, then sets a finger to her lips, glancing towards the study. She crosses to sit in the armchair.*)

FAITH   (*throatily*) I see. I see. Here to read the Will. I
                 see.

BLUNDELL   Indeed, Madam.

FAITH   Then let us waste no further time. Call in the
                 servants, Miss Beale.

                 (*Descending the stairs,* ANNE *exits* L.)

                 You did mention in your letters – about
                 having the servants present?

BLUNDELL   The ah, employees, yes. That would be
                 correct.

MICKLEBY   (*urgent whisper*) Mr Blundell ..

BLUNDELL   The briefcase, Mr Mickleby, if you please.

                 (*Glowering,* MICKLEBY *collects the briefcase* BC,
                 and shoves it under BLUNDELL'S *arms. Then he
                 returns* BC *for the little chair.*)

FAITH   My stepfather left minor keepsakes---baubels-
                 --to these servants?

BLUNDELL   The employees are mentioned, yes.

                 (*The Staff enter* L: *first is* AGNES *the Lancashire
                 Cook, elderly and motherly in black coat over her
                 white uniform. The others follow her in.*)

FAITH   Come in! Come in! Seat yourselves and settle
                 down.

                 (*The three ladies share the sofa.* AGNES C, MABEL
                 R *and* ANNE L. JOHNSON *is the last to enter, and
                 he stands behind the sofa.*)

                 (*Off-handedly*) That is Agnes the Cook, Mabel
                 the maid, Miss Beale, and Johnson . . . a
                 chauffeur.

BLUNDELL   Afternoon ladies; Mr Johnson.

MICKLEBY   Yes, 'afternoon. Dreadful day. Terrible and
                 everything.

(*Bringing the chair to* C, MICKLEBY *whispers desperately into* BLUNDELL'S *ear.*)

You can't, Uncle. Sacrilege. Madness. Must tell them . . .

(*Everyone stares at him. He smirks weakly.* BLUNDELL *slams down the chair.*)

BLUNDELL   I trust you may forgive my nephew. He was overcome by emotion.

FAITH   Perhaps he should remember it is *I* who have suffered the loss.

MICKLEBY: Yes, M'am —— (*Glancing at the study.*) —— just what I was thinking.

(BLUNDELL *sits, sets spectacles upon his nose, clears his throat, and reads.*)

BLUNDELL   "This is the Last Will and Testament of Charles Barraclough. I, Charles Barraclough, being of sound mind, do hereby direct that my estate be divided equally between my stepdaughters Faith and Hope . . .

FAITH   (*pleased*) Ah.

BLUNDELL   "with the exception of certain bequests detailed hereunder." You are named as executrix, Miss Barraclough. Can you contact your sister?

FAITH   Yes yes yes. What about these people?

BLUNDELL   "In appreciation of their faithful service and generous friendship, my employees are to receive the following legacies . . .

FAITH   (*shocked*) Legacies?

BLUNDELL   Legacies, Madam. (*Reads.*) "On the understanding they do not resign their positions until six months after my death." (*Adjusts spectacles.*)

(*The listeners lean forward in suspense.*)

(*Reads.*) "Agnes my cheery Cook, seven thousand pounds".

AGNES   Ee, bless his heart.

MICKLEBY   Congratulations. Jolly good.

BLUNDELL   "Anne Beale, seven thousand pounds."

(ANNE *remains calm, looks at her hands.*)

MICKLEBY   Congratulations. Jolly good.

BLUNDELL   "Ted Johnson, two thousand pounds."

MICKLEBY   Congrat —— oh hard luck.

(JOHNSON *slaps his first and turns upstage.*)

BLUNDELL   "And Mabel Middy, seven thousand pounds."

MABEL   Wheee! (*Rising, she kisses* MICKLEBY *impulsively, then sits again.*)

MICKLEBY   Oh thank you. (*Aside to* BLUNDELL.) Pity it wasn't ten thousand.

(FAITH *rises in fury. She snatches the Will.*)

FAITH   It's outrageous! (*Reading avidly.*) Monstrous. I'll contest it.

BLUNDELL   Madam, I do beg you . . .

FAITH   No one'll steal my money. It's mine. I've waited a lifetime.

(*She rips the document to pieces.*)

It's mine! . . . Mine! . . . Mine! . . . Mine!

(*Uproar!* FAITH *throws down the torn pieces, then falls into her chair, gasping.*)

BLUNDELL   Madam. Really. Please. This is most unorthodox . . .

(*He and* MICKLEBY *drop to their knees, clucking and collecting the shredded Will.* FAITH *shouts across them at her employees.*)

FAITH You all think you've beaten me, but you're wrong. The money's only yours if you do not resign within six months. Well you won't have the chance. I'm dismissing you ... (*Triumphantly.*) ... all of you. Now!

BLUNDELL Ah, we cannot advise that, Madam.

FAITH Who's going to stop me? You've had your say.

BLUNDELL Not quite, madam. I have yet to read a further Condition.

MICKLEBY Yes. In several parts.

(MICKLEBY *rises, helps* BLUNDELL *into the chair, stands* R *of him, and hands him a jagged piece of torn will.*)

BLUNDELL (*reads*) "My employees are to receive their wages, board and keep, as up to the time of my death ...

(MICKLEBY *hands him a smaller piece.*)

"and ... "

(*He glowers at* MICKLEBY, *who hands him a larger bit.*)

"may not be dismissed ... "

(MICKLEBY *hands him a fragment.*)

"Full stop."

(BLUNDELL *puts the pieces on the table.* MICKLEBY *scoops them into the briefcase.*)

FAITH (*hissing*) I am to support his parasites.

BLUNDELL (*monotone from memory*) "Signed by the said Testator in the presence of us, present at the same time ... "

FAITH | We hated him ... (*rising, circling to behind her armchair*) ... and all the menials he gathered around him. He knew we hated him ... and he's done this to mock us from the grave. But I'm not finished. If it takes every penny ... I'll ... my throat ... !

(*She clutches her throat, swaying.* MICKLEBY *moves up to support her.*)

Something wrong ... poisoned! ... I've been poisoned.

(BLUNDELL, MABEL *and* AGNES *rise.* ANNE *remains seated.*)

That tea ... tasted bitter. *She* poisoned me. ... Anne Beale ... !

(FAITH *staggers between* BLUNDELL *and* MICKLEBY, *pointing a palsied finger.* ANNE *rises and moves to* JOHNSON *behind the sofa.*)

Anne Beale. ... I know why ... I know ... ...

(*She collapses into the solicitors' arms.*)

MICKLEBY | Oh good Lord. Oh dear.

BLUNDELL | Is there, ah, somewhere ah ... ?

JOHNSON | There's a divan in the study. I'll show you.

(*He exits* R. BLUNDELL *and* MICKLEBY *follow him, half-carrying* FAITH. MICKLEBY *returns quickly.*)

MICKLEBY | Mabel, brandy some bring ... bring some brand ... brangy brangy ... (*Deep breath.*) Cognac! (*He exits* R.)

MABEL | Yes, sir. Righto, sir. Righto. (*Runs out* C.)

AGNES | (*suddenly, loudly wailing*) Eeee, s-s-seven thou-thousand pounds ...

ANNE	(*pats her shoulder*) Weeping? You should be laughing, Agnes.
AGNES	Aye. And so should you.
ANNE	*I* handed her the tea.
AGNES	*I* made it.

(*They give each other a quick look.*)

Suppose there's no harm in having a little laugh. (*She beams broadly, then her face drops.*) But . . . s-seven thou--ou-sand p-pounds . . . eeee!

(AGNES *exits* L, *wailing louder than ever.* ANNE *sits on the sofa, hands to her face.*)

JOHNSON	Careful. Keep strong! (*He crosses to sit beside her.*)
ANNE	It's too late.
JOHNSON	Darling, she was hysterical. Who'd believe her.
ANNE	(*shakes her head*) It's too late. She accused me.
JOHNSON	Trust in me, darlin'. I'll see you through.

(*He cups her face and kisses her. But we are never sure if* JOHNSON'S *charm is good or evil.*)

MICKLEBY	(*enters* R) Oh! Having a bit of fun? Ha ha. Excuse me. 'Fraid we'll need the family sawbones.
JOHNSON	(*rises*) Dr Brown's his name. (*Nods at the desk.*) The telephone lady'll get you the number.
MICKLEBY	(*moves to the desk* R) Oh, got one of these, have you?

(*He sits at the desk and lifts the receiver of the antique telephone.*)

JOHNSON	How is Miss Barraclough, sir?

MICKLEBY	Still out. Feel a bit dicky myself.
	(BLUNDELL *enters slowly.* MABEL *hurries in* C. *carrying brandy in a glass.*)
MABEL	This'll bring her round.
BLUNDELL	I fear nothing will do that. Miss Barraclough is dead.
	(*Long mournful howl from the dog, off.*)
MICKLEBY	(*into receiver, brightly*) hello, operator? . . . (*Glumly.*) Goodbye!
	(MICKLEBY *rises.* ANNE *starts to rise, but* JOHNSON *stops her.* BLUNDELL *returns the Will-reading chair back to its position in front of the panel.*)
BLUNDELL	She died without regaining consciousness.
	(*During a pause, uncomfortable for all of them,* BLUNDELL *comes back to the end of the sofa.* MICKLEBY *and* MABEL *are together.*)
MABEL	I had a feeling all the time . . . watching eyes . . . eyes watching . . . watching.
	(*She looks round the room, ending up face-to-face with* MICKLEBY. *The latter finds himself looking cross-eyed at her. He shakes his head and turns away.*)
BLUNDELL	Miss, Beale. Ah, is it true Miss Barraclough complained about her tea? (*Sits on sofa.*)
ANNE	Yes. She did.
BLUNDELL	(*consulting his pocket watch*) How long ago was this.
ANNE	Three o'clock or just after.
JOHNSON	She was hysterical, anyone could see.
	(BLUNDELL *looks upwards into* JOHNSON'S *belligerent face.*)
BLUNDELL	Oh yes. Ah yes, of course.

JOHNSON   Then cut out the trick questions.

BLUNDELL   By all means. Yes.

           (BLUNDELL *rises hurriedly and retires to the foot of the stairs.*)

ANNE   Mr Blundell is wondering what happened to the cup.

BLUNDELL   Well, yes. Ha ha. I was, s'matter of fact.

MABEL   (*moving to* BLUNDELL) I washed it up. But don't start looking at me!

BLUNDELL   No, no! Anything but!

MICKLEBY   (*moves up to* MABEL) Oh ha, ha, ha! Just one of those little mysteries, I expect. I mean, there's no proof the lady *was* poisoned. In any case, nobody here would would ... And even if they had, it ... it ... (*Quickly.*) D'you mind, dear!

           (MICKLEBY *grabs the brandy from* MABEL, *downs it in a gulp and hands back the glass.*)

ANNE   I'm sure you gentlemen will be in need of refreshment.

MICKLEBY   Not in this house!

BLUNDELL   Thank you, Miss Beale. Please don't bother.

ANNE   (*moving to the stairs*) It's no bother. Mabel, will you tell Cook?

MABEL   Righto, dear. (*Exits* C.)

ANNE   Excuse me.

           (JOHNSON *moves up to* BLUNDELL, *menacingly.*)

JOHNSON   Any more questions?

           (BLUNDELL *pulls* MICKLEBY *between himself and the Chauffeur.*)

BLUNDELL   Any more questions, Mr Mickleby?

MICKLEBY	No, no. No!
ANNE	(*paused on stairs*) Ted!
	(JOHNSON *gives the men a sinister look then follows* ANNE *upstairs.*)
BLUNDELL	(*to the telephone*) Well! 'Better telephone the doctor again. Certificates and all that.
	(MABEL *appears silently (from* C *opening) behind* MICKLEBY.)
MABEL	I knew . . . . .
MICKLEBY	Aaaagh! (*Swings round to face her.*)
MABEL	Sorry. . . . I knew something horrid'd 'appen. Said as much when you arrived, didn't I, Mr Muckleby.
MICKLEBY	Mickleby, actually. Anyway, all over now, eh!
	(MICKLEBY *backs away from her during all this.* MABEL *follows, speaking in spine-chilling tones.*)
MABEL	No, that's the trouble. I still feel the same.
MICKLEBY	You d-d-do?
	(*He leans against the armchair, but the chair isn't where he thought it was. He staggers backwards and bumps into* BLUNDELL *who is seated by the telephone.*)
MABEL	You mark my words, sir. We haven't finished with *death!*
MICKLEBY	Aaagh!
	(*He grips* BLUNDELL'S *neck.*)
BLUNDELL	Aaagh!
	(BLUNDELL *pushes* MICKLEBY *away – looking at him aghast.*)
MICKLEBY	Sorry, sir.
	(MABEL *goes up to the centre opening, and turns.*)

MABLE	There's a guest room in the hall if you gentlemen'd care to ... wash your hands. S'pect you'll be dying to by now. (*She exits.*)
MICKLEBY	(*into* BLUNDELL'S *ear*) Mr Blundell. The police. Fast!
BLUNDELL	Ssh! Hang on to this whilst I'm thinking.

(BLUNDELL *holds out the telephone, hands wide, with the receiver in his right and the mouthpiece in his left.* MICKLEBY (*who is behind* BLUNDELL'S *chair*) *grabs the instrument from* BLUNDELL, *but gets the cord trapped round* BLUNDELL'S *throat, almost strangling him.*)

Fool!

MICKLEBY	Sorry, sir.

(BLUNDELL *rises, collects the briefcase from the table and sits on the sofa.*)

(*into phone*) Oh! Hello, Operator? Could you put me through to the local doctor, please? Dr Brown? ... (*Very quickly.*) Oh has he? Oh did he? Oh would you? Oh thank you. (*Pause.* BLUNDELL *looks at him.*) Doctor's at the Undertakers.

BLUNDELL	Who killed *him*?
MICKLEBY	Nobody. The Undertaker's having a baby. And that's how *I* feel. (*Into the receiver, cheerily.*) Hello! Is that the Undertak ..... I mean, (*gloomily*) is that the Undertaker? Could I speak to Dr Brow .... Oh has he? Oh did he? Oh would you? Oh thank you. (*Pause.* BLUNDELL *looks at him again.*) The Doctor's on his way *here*. (*Into phone.*) He is!? He didn't! You didn't! Did you? Well done! (*To* BLUNDELL.) It's twins. Six pounds each.
BLUNDELL	Think twice next time, won't he!

MICKLEBY   Yes. (*Into phone.*) You'll think twice next . . .

             (MICKLEBY *checks himself, and hangs up with a quick "Goodbye". Then he crosses to sit* L *of* BLUNDELL *on the sofa.*)

             The Doctor'll know about poisoned tea. And yet I can't believe that nice Anne Beale's a poisoner.

BLUNDELL   Y'never know. Look at Abilgail Taylor. Picture of purity at the trial . . . but she stabbed Mr Taylor ten times with a potato peeler.

MICKLEBY   Poor old Spud!

BLUNDELL   But where does the missing body come in?

MICKLEBY   Don't ask me. Hope he's staying out.

BLUNDELL   Who pinched Mr Barraclough and why? Where've they put him; and how?

             (MABEL *enters silently* DL, *carrying a tray with two cups and saucers and one spoon. She moves behind (and between) the two men.*)

MABEL   'Scuse me!

             (*Both men jump in surprise.* MABEL *leans forward, offering the tray between the two men. They each take a cup.*)

             You'll be dying for a cup of tea.

MICKLEBY   "Dying"?

MABEL   Cook's making some sandwiches.

BLUNDELL   Oh, not to worry. Thank you. This tea'll do us.

             (*On 'do us'* MICKLEBY *and* BLUNDELL *exchange glances.* MICKLEBY, *his eyes fixed on* MABEL, *starts stirring his tea, but the spoon is outside his cup.* BLUNDELL *puts* MICKLEBY'S *hand in the correct position. But* MICKLEBY *is stirring so violently and his hand is shaking so much,* MICKLEBY *has to hold down his cup.*)

BLUNDELL	Give me the spoon!

(BLUNDELL *moves* MICKLEBY'S *hand towards his own cup . . . but instead of leaving the spoon in his uncle's cup,* MICKLEBY *leaves his own cup on top of* BLUNDELL'S, *retains the spoon, and continues stirring his empty saucer.*)

(MABEL *creeps to the door* L, *then pessimistically.*)

MABEL Well, I hope you enjoy it! (*Exits.*)

MICKLEBY Didn't much care for that last look she gave us.

BLUNDELL Nonsense! We don't know Madam *was* poisoned . . . yet.

MICKLEBY N—no.

BLUNDELL Anyway, there's no proof it was the tea.

MICKLEBY No.

BLUNDELL Well then!

(*They raise cups to their lips, unhappily, simultaneously, and after a pause – during which they sneak peeps at each other.*)

BLUNDELL On the other hand!

MICKLEBY Exactly!

(*After "Exactly", they quickly lower their cups in unison.*)

BLUNDELL Mind you, it's silly to worry, of course.

MICKLEBY Oh yes, yes.

BLUNDELL But there might be somewhere in the washroom we could pour this.

MICKLEBY I know the very place.

(MICKLEBY *and* BLUNDELL *exit* C *purposefully.*
JOHNSON *hurries down the stairs. He takes a quick
glance into the hall, then crosses furtively to the
desk* R. *In one of the drawers he discovers a
revolver, and moves to the staircase. Here he holds
the gun to the light and checks it is loaded.* ANNE
appears on the stairs.)

ANNE	Ted! They'll catch you.
JOHNSON	We'll have to chance that. (*Returns to desk.*)
ANNE	Not now! Later.
JOHNSON	(*searching*) Later may be *too* late.

(ANNE *moves to the bottom step.*)

ANNE	(*urgently whispering*) No, Ted! I'm frightened.
JOHNSON	Darling, will you leave this to me!
ANNE	I feel so guilty, and I can't pretend I'm not. Can't disguise my eyes.
JOHNSON	Don't say things like that!

(*He moves to her and swings her round to face
him.*)

ANNE	They'll call the police.
JOHNSON	Not until the Doctor's been. There's still time.
ANNE	"You poisoned me", she said. The last words of a dying woman.
JOHNSON	It was heart failure, like her father. Now get that straight!
ANNE	(*moves to above the sofa*) God, if only it hadn't happened. If only.
JOHNSON	(*following*) If only we hadn't nine thousand, as well? Nine thousand, darling. Think of it! Dream of it.
ANNE	Ted, you must tell me the truth.

JOHNSON   Anne, I've to work fast now. You leave me.
            I'll fix everything.

            (*He leads her to the kitchen door where she turns.*)

ANNE   Old Mr Barraclough – swear to me, Ted,
            swear you didn't kill him.

            (JOHNSON *kisses her violently before she can say
            more.* BLUNDELL *and* MICKLEBY *appear* C.
            BLUNDELL *tugs* MICKLEBY *back, then they peep
            carefully.*)

ANNE   Dr Brown'll know.

JOHNSON   Dr Brown is an old dodderer. He wouldn't
            recognise poison if he saw it. (*Kisses her
            briefly.*) Now hop it!

            (ANNE *exits.* JOHNSON *hurries back to the desk.*
            BLUNDELL *moves into the room, and to behind the
            armchair.* MICKLEBY *follows. Suddenly* JOHNSON
            *becomes aware that someone is behind him. He
            straightens up, snapping closed the little chest lid.
            Then he swings round.*)

BLUNDELL   Hello there!

JOHNSON   I . . . I was looking for an envelope. Miss
            Faith used to keep them in this chest.

BLUNDELL   Oh yes?

JOHNSON   Yes. (*Crosses* L.) Excuse me.

BLUNDELL   Oh, Mr Johnson! Perhaps someone'd kindly
            inform us when Dr Brown arrives.

JOHNSON   Sure, but he'll walk straight in. You'll see him
            all right.

BLUNDELL   Splendid.

JOHNSON   You may find him strange at first. He's not
            English, he just calls himself Brown.

BLUNDELL   Really?

JOHNSON	(*moving closer to them*) Yes, and he's deaf, and short-sighted, and absent-minded. But he's a very good doctor.
	(MICKLEBY *looks quickly at* BLUNDELL.)
BLUNDELL	(*corner of his mouth*) Sounds as though *he* needs a good doctor!
	(*Thunder, lightning. The lights flicker.*)
JOHNSON	It's awful violent on the moors in winter. Lost two hikers last year.
MICKLEBY	Lost?
JOHNSON	(*leaning closer*) Sucked into the marshes. Could happen to anyone.
	(MICKLEBY *gulps with a sucking sound.*)
	(*Brightly.*) Shall I drive your car into the garage?
MICKLEBY	No thanks, old boy. Just leave it, if you don't mind... preferably with the engine running.
JOHNSON	You'll not be staying then?
MICKLEBY	Oh no no no.
BLUNDELL	We may have to, for a while.
JOHNSON	Oh. Well, I suppose Mabel could always fix you a bed. In the late Mr Barraclough's room.
	(*Dog howl.* JOHNSON *turns and walks to the door* L.)
MICKLEBY	Would that be the room where he...?
JOHNSON	Died, yes. Three nights ago at twelve.
	(*The old bell clangs once.*)
BLUNDELL	Thank you, we shan't be staying. We've ah, pressing business in town.
MICKLEBY	Couple of shrouds to iron. (*Weakly.*) Ha ha.

JOHNSON   Many a true word, sir. (*Exits.*)

BLUNDELL   That young fella would like us gone

MICKLEBY   Me, too. (*Clutching* BLUNDELL's *jacket.*) Uncle, we've read the Will. Let's be gone.

BLUNDELL   Sit down, Hubert. And leave go my jacket.

MICKLEBY   Wanted to be near someone warm for a change. (*Sits on* R *end of the sofa.*)

BLUNDELL   So! Brown is a good doctor yet a bad doctor. (*Moves thoughtfully to the desk.*) And there's a link between Anne Beale and Johnson. Mmm, intriguing. And what about Johnson? Fiddling with his Mistress's chest.

MICKLEBY   Pardon?

BLUNDELL   This box here.

MICKLEBY   Oh! Yes.

             (BLUNDELL *turns upstage, not noticing the arrival of* DR BROWN. DR BROWN *is an eccentric of pop bottle spectacles, grey beard, exploding hair, rain hat, tweed cape and carpet slippers. Peering shortsightedly, he pads to* C *and places his bag where he thinks the table should be. His bag drops to the floor.*)

BLUNDELL   (*hearing the bang*) Ah, Dr Brown?

             (DR BROWN *pads to the sofa and sits.* MICKELBY *slides from beneath, him just in time.*

MICKLEBY   Dr Brown? (*Taps his shoulder.*)

DOCTOR   Himmel, I am not knowink peoples are here.

             (*He peers at* MICKLEBY, *speaking in a fractured indeterminate foreign accent.*)

             You are come to the funeral? Gut. The Undertaker's babies I am just delivered.

(BLUNDELL *draws closed the* BC *curtains, then moves to the sofa.*)

BLUNDELL	Yes, indeed. Six pounds each.
DOCTOR	(*cups his ear at* MICKLEBY) Beg to pardon?
BLUNDELL	Six pounds.
DOCTOR	No, National Health.
MICKLEBY	He's wearing slippers, too.
DOCTOR	The floods is shockink. Cats'n dogs? Elephants it is rainink.
BLUNDELL	I fear we've had rather a tragedy, sir.
DOCTOR	Beg to pardon?

(DR BROWN *again cups his ear at* MICKLEBY, *who points a guiding finger. He follows* MICKLEBY'S *finger until he sees* BLUNDELL.)

Himmel! More peoples.

BLUNDELL	(*loudly*) Miss Barraclough is dead.
DOCTOR	Not to worry, I shouldn't. Put oil in the ears, then syringe.
BLUNDELL	(*louder*) But she is dead.
DOCTOR	(*at* MICKLEBY *again*) Beg to pardon?
MICKLEBY	He's back again.
BLUNDELL	(*yells*) Dea-ea-ead!
DOCTOR	Ach, so is I. She should grumble at her age. (*Rises.*) As you wish. Please to point me in the general direction.
BLUNDELL	In the study, Doctor.
DOCTOR	Gut. Gut. Peace and quiet she must have. Too much is hurry and bustlink these days. (*He bumps into the table.* BLUNDELL *steers him gently* R *handing him his bag.*) Oh! She are in the study. Thank you, younk woman.

DOCTOR   (*pauses at the door*) Now I want you should
              don't worry. I shall have her up and about in
              no time. (*He exits* R.)

MICKLEBY   If there has been a murder, I reckon he did
              it.

BLUNDELL   Why?

MICKLEBY   He's the most unlikely.

BLUNDELL   Hubert-m'boy, something smells at
              Greenacres. A missing corpse, a dead woman,
              and five beneficiaries to a fortune.

              (BLUNDELL *paces round and round the armchair.*
              Rising, MICKLEBY *follows him around.*)

MICKLEBY   Not five, it's six.

BLUNDELL   Five beneficiaries.

MICKLEBY   No, sir. Six.

BLUNDELL   Don't argue, sir. (*Counts on his fingers.*)
              There's Anne Beale. There's Johnson your
              chauffeur, Mabel your maid, Agnes your
              cook and there's the other sister. Five!

              (*Eyes widened in dread.* MICKLEBY *dashes to the*
              sofa, empties out the pieces of torn will from his
              briefcase, and shuffles them frantically.)

MICKLEBY   Oh good Lord. Oh dear. Oh no. Oh please.

BLUNDELL   (*crosses to him*) What's up? What's wrong?. . .
              Cease babbling, Mr Mickleby. Tell me!

MICKLEBY   You read out the wrong will.

BLUNDELL   I WHAT? (*He snatches the grubby fragments.*)

MICKLEBY   He was always changing them, Uncle-sir-Mr
              Blundell. They arrived at the office like
              circulars. That one's last month's.

BLUNDELL	You're joking, Hubert. This is one of your jolly leg-pulls, aha-ha-ha-ha-ha. Yes, isn't it?
MICKLEBY	(*nods, laughing inanely*) No. . . . I'm sure I posted that copy back to Barraclough and filed the new will. Somebody must have swapped them.
BLUNDELL	(*aghast*) You stood by, allowing me to read an obsolete Will?
MICKLEBY	I wasn't listening. I was too worried over the missing corpse.
BLUNDELL	Oh no! (*Sinks on to the sofa.*) Sic Transit! . . . Habeas Corpus . . . Homo Sapiens . . . Amen.
MICKLEBY	(*kneels beside him*) We could phone town and get the office copy.
BLUNDELL	It's Saturday, you Nit!
MICKLEBY	(*tiny voice*) Sorry, Mr Blundell.
BLUNDELL	(*rising*) It's horrifying . . . fantastic. The possibilities are too dreadful to consider. We'll be drummed out of Lincoln's Inn.
MICKLEBY	Oh don't.
BLUNDELL	It's never happened before. D'you know what you've done?
MICKLEBY	Made history.
BLUNDELL	Don't speak to me! Don't ever speak to me again. (*Dramatically.*) And I – shall never speak to you. (BLUNDELL *sinks into the armchair and, for a second, buries his head in his hands. Pause.*) How did the Wills differ?
MICKLEBY	Oh, thank you, sir.
	(*Picking up the briefcase from the sofa, he hurries over and kneels beside* BLUNDELL'S *chair, whispering urgently, secretly.*)

	Almost the same, sir, really sir. The employees still got their money. Just one more beneficiary, that's all.
BLUNDELL	And who was it? — as if I didn't know you'd forgotten.
MICKLEBY	That's right.
BLUNDELL	Think, man! Think!
MICKLEBY	Wait! I think the name was ....
BLUNDELL	Yes?
MICKLEBY	Don't laugh, will you.
BLUNDELL	(*screeches*) Hubert, I shall break into uncontrollable sobs.
MICKLEBY	Well, sir, I think the name was Nikkamoppaloffkis.
BLUNDELL	Nikka ...? Oh, let me die. Miss, Mrs or Mister? (MICKLEBY *shrugs*.) You remember a name like that, and not the sex?
MICKLEBY	Nikkamoppaloffkis, that's all.

(BLUNDELL *rises, dragging* MICKLEBY *to his feet.*)

BLUNDELL	It's a court case! Misrepresentation! Criminal negligence! Worse! If she wasn't poisoned, it could've been heart failure — because *we* read the wrong Will! (*He shakes* MICKLEBY'S *shoulders*.) We're guilty of technical manslaughter — worth anything up to ten years apiece.
MICKLEBY	We'll need a good solicitor.

(BLUNDELL *releases* MICKLEBY *and strides to the telephone.*)

BLUNDELL	I'll try and contact Mr Weatherby. In the meantime, Hubert, pray. Pray, Hubert!

(MICKLEBY *clasps his hands and gazes upwards.*)

MICKLEBY   Oh Lord. With reference to my Clanger of
                the Twenty-Third ultimo, and the
                circumstances ensuing therefrom ......

BLUNDELL   Check that briefcase again!

MICKLEBY   (*eyes upwards*) Got to check the briefcase.
                Amen.

                (MICKLEBY *retrieves the briefcase from the floor by
                the armchair. There is nothing inside it.*)

BLUNDELL   (*into phone*) Hello? Ah, young lady, I want a
                call to London, please: Holborn 714 ... This
                is Grange 13. (*In horror.*) Thirteen. (*To
                MICKLEBY.*) Anything?

MICKLEBY   Nothing, sir. (*He moves close to* BLUNDELL DR.)

BLUNDELL   There's a possible motive here: another
                suspect. Nikkamoppa .... oh blast! At this
                very moment he could be lacing the tea
                caddy with cyanide. (*Into the phone.*) Hello,
                Weatherby? ... Oh thank heavens!

MICKLEBY   Thank heavens! (*Presses his ear close to the
                telephone.*)

BLUNDELL   (*into phone*) Look, I cannot explain now, but
                we must have a copy of the latest
                Barraclough Will. ... Blundell! Mr
                Blundell. ... Be a good fellow and dash to
                the office for it, would you? ... I know. I'm
                sorry, but you could do it in an hour and
                ring us back. ... Grange 13 ... Oh
                grand! ... (*To* MICKLEBY.) What's it filed
                under? B for Barraclough?

MICKLEBY   No. W.

BLUNDELL   (*into phone*) It's filed under ... (*Back to his
                nephew.*) It's filed under *what*?

MICKLEBY   W for Will.

BLUNDELL   (*into phone.*) Mr Mickleby has filed it under W
for Will. You'd better check S for
Shakespeare, too.

(MICKLEBY *stares at his uncle with self-righteous
mystification.*)

BLUNDELL   (*into phone*) Right ... About an
hour. ... Thank you very much. Goodbye.

(*He replaces the receiver and advances ominously
towards* MICKLEBY — *who backs away.*)

MICKLEBY   Now now, Mr Blundell.

BLUNDELL   I ought to tear off your ears, roll them into
little balls, and ...

MICKLEBY   No, Uncle. Pax. Pax.

BLUNDELL   There *is* a mystery here. I'm going to solve it
and you are going to help me.

MICKLEBY   Yes, Mr Blundell.

BLUNDELL   No more yelping for policemen. They're the
last people we need now.

MICKLEBY   Yes, Mr Blundell.

BLUNDELL   Our only chance is to hope that poor woman
was poisoned ... and find who did it.

MICKLEBY   Yes, Mr Blundell.

BLUNDELL   Then find the missing body.

MICKLEBY   Yes, Mr Blundell.

BLUNDELL   Then your Will botch-up might be forgiven.

MICKLEBY   Be wonderful Mr Blunderful.

(*The lights flicker and go out. All is black.*)

Uncle, it's gone d-d-dark.

BLUNDELL Be darker than this in prison. I wonder what Miss Faith would have said, had she known about this?

(*Thunder* Lightning. *The centre curtains are draw open with a frightening swi-i-ish, and the ghost of* FAITH BARRACLOUGH *seemingly glides towards them.*)

THE FIGURE About what?

(*The two solicitors turn and see her.* MICKLEBY *faints into* BLUNDELL'S *arms.*)

MUSIC CURTAIN

ACT ONE
Scene Two

Ten Minutes Later.

HOPE BARRACLOUGH, *mistaken for the ghost of her sister in the previous Scene is dressed similarly to* FAITH. *She should be as alike as possible in appearance, veiled and black-garbed. In manner, she is given to the same bursts of fury, yet enjoys sarcasm and delivers acid remarks with a cold fixed smile.*

When the curtain rises, BLUNDELL *and* MICKLEBY *are standing behind the sofa, fascinated by* HOPE ... *who has her back to the audience right down* C. *As she speaks, she sweeps upstage and round in a circle.*

HOPE This room is filled with astral music and joyous spirit voices. Beside us now with smiling countenance are two children – my stepfather and my sister Faith.

(BLUNDELL *and* MICKLEBY *exchange quizzical glances.*)

Now they are flying to blissful eternity,
turning for one last farewell. (*She gazes into
'eternity' out front.*) Goodbye, dear children,
goodbye.

(MICKLEBY *waves.* BLUNDELL *slaps his hand.*
HOPE *sits in the armchair, daintily touching a
handkerchief to her eyes.*)

HOPE   Please forgive me. I realise how strange this
            must seem to unbelievers.

BLUNDELL   Indeed no, Madame. I can only apologise
            once again for our unfortunate behaviour
            upon your arrival. (*He glowers at* MICKLEBY.)

(MICKLEBY *tries to laugh obligingly.*)

BLUNDELL   Miss Barraclough, I understand no one has
            contacted you regarding your stepfather's sad
            ah, demise.

HOPE   I've been in seclusion.

BLUNDELL   Yet here you are – dressed, ah, for the
            funeral.

HOPE   So I am.

BLUNDELL   May I enquire how you heard the unhappy
            news?

HOPE   I received the Call. (*Rising.*) Three nights ago
            at twelve o'clock I awoke to find a trumpet
            hovering over my pillow.

MICKLEBY   A trumpet?

HOPE   A spiritual manifestation.

MICKLEBY   Louis Armstrong. I'm off!

(*He starts towards* L. BLUNDELL *pulls him back*
HOPE *moves swiftly to them.*)

HOPE   I am embarrassing you, Mr Mickleby?

MICKLEBY   No, no.

HOPE	But you see, we believe mortal tragedy is merely an introduction to ethereal ecstacy.
MICKLEBY	Yes, I'm sure it is.
HOPE	Though, naturally, I am shocked to have lost my dear sister. Poison, did you say?
BLUNDELL	Ah, well, as yet there is no proof.
HOPE	In any case, Death is the great Peacemaker, is it not?
MICKLEBY	Bit late to start a quarrel.
BLUNDELL	Um yes. We haven't informed the Police, I fear.
HOPE	Oh, I'm so glad. They do trample one's carpets, do they not! (*She plucks a hair from* BLUNDELL's *jacket.*) Please be seated, gentlemen.

(*The men demur.*)

Sit when I ask you!

(*The men do so quickly, on the upstage side of the sofa, backs to the audience.* BLUNDELL *on the* R *end.* MICKLEBY's *arm creeps round his Uncle's waist for comfort.* BLUNDELL *slaps it away.*)

My sister was given to dramatics, you know. Had there been some un-natural reason for her death, I should have sensed the vibrations.

(*She moves around below the sofa.* BLUNDELL *rises and follows her.*)

Yet I feel only an atmosphere of happy release.

BLUNDELL	Miss Barraclough, ah, I am concerned about how we're going to reach the truth of the matter.
HOPE	(*swings round angrily*) Why? Why?

BLUNDELL	Well, Dr Brown seems hardly ah, ...
HOPE	(*angrily*) The Family will hear nothing against Dr Brown, Mr Blundell!
BLUNDELL	I beg you pardon, M'am.

(*He sits on the downstage side of the sofa. There is a bang and we realise he has knocked* MICKLEBY *off the upstage side.* MICKLEBY *picks himself up and stands* C.)

HOPE	When I first arrived, you babbled something about missing beneficiaries.
BLUNDELL	(*half rises*) An unforgiveable error, Madam. We read out the wrong Will.
HOPE	Did you say why? I've forgotten.
MICKLEBY	I b-brought an obsolete copy from the office. (*He giggles nervously.*) Terribly sorry, M'am. Can't think how it happened. Impossible, really, but I did it. (*Giggles.*) Don't know how. (*Giggles again.*)
HOPE	Why are you laughing?
MICKLEBY	I don't know that, either.

(*He sits on* BLUNDELL'S *lap in mistake for the sofa ... Then sits next to him.*)

BLUNDELL	We are expecting a telephone communication with the relevant details, M'am. We're abjectly sorry.

(HOPE *moves round and stands above the sofa, immediately behind them.*)

HOPE	We *could* ignore your contretemps.
BLUNDELL MICKLEBY	} (*delightedly together*) Oh, thank you!
HOPE	But we cannot –.
BLUNDELL MICKLEBY	} (*dejectedly*) Oh!

HOPE	– should a policeman require details.
BLUNDELL MICKLEBY	} (*groaning*) Oh.
HOPE	(*returns to* C) What would happen if the servants *did* resign within six months?
BLUNDELL	(*rises*) Their money would revert to you, Madam.
HOPE	Really! Not that I begrudge the poor dears their legacies. But it's a strange world . . . anything may happen.

(*The dog howls.*)

DOCTOR	(*entering* R) Are anybody here?
HOPE	Dr Brown! Dear Doctor!

(*Hope meets* DR BROWN BC. *The* DOCTOR *peers at* HOPE, *looks back at the study, then again at her.*)

DOCTOR	Ah! Feelink better?

(BLUNDELL *slaps his head in exasperation, then moves around behind the sofa to sit on the upstage right corner of the sofa.*)

HOPE	I am Hope, Doctor. I am the sister of Faith.
DOCTOR	(*peering closely*) Tush, tush, so you is! (*Takes her hand.*) So dreadful sorry, dreadful. Poor poor lady.
HOPE	What was the cause of death?
DOCTOR	So very younk. Heart failure.
MICKLEBY	(*whispers*) We're Guilty!
BLUNDELL	Sssh! (*He rises and moves in.*)
DOCTOR	I am not knowink the heart are weak. Most strange, yet. (*Nods.*) Ya, heart failure.
HOPE	(*significantly*) Heart failure, Mr Blundell.

BLUNDELL	Yes.
DOCTOR	Let I consider – who are the elder sister, yet?
HOPE	I was, Doctor, by three minutes.
DOCTOR	Ach ya! There are a slight contusion of the umbillicum in your case. No matter. I shall look at it later.

(*He moves happily to the study door, knocks and waits.*)

HOPE	Go straight in, Doctor! My sister will not mind.
DOCTOR	(*speaking into the study*) Ah! Havink a little snooze? (*He exits.*)
HOPE	You seem disappointed, Mr Blundell.
BLUNDELL	Miss Barraclough, I strongly advise a second medical opinion.
HOPE	And I advise you, Mr Blundell, to return to London. (*She lowers her veil.*)
MICKLEBY	Oh marvellous!

(*He rises and moves to* C, *but* BLUNDELL *pushes him back . . . .* MICKLEBY *sits on the* R *end of the sofa in deep gloom.*)

BLUNDELL	Ah! – there is the telephone information we are expecting.
HOPE	Oh yes. A nuisance.

(MABEL *enters wearing an apron over her black dress and carrying a plate of sandwiches.*)

MABEL	Cook insisted I bring these sandwiches.

(*Upon seeing the veiled* HOPE, *she utters a strangled howl. Her plate droops, and its sandwiches slide into* MICKLEBY'S *lap. Darting forward,* BLUNDELL *catches* MABEL *as she faints. He eases her on to the u/s* L *end of the sofa.*)

(MICKLEBY *rises into a crouched position, and, cuddling the sandwiches, wanders to* C *like a refugee from a Slavonic dance.*)

(BLUNDELL *takes* MABEL'S *plate, and wafts her with it. Then moving to* MICKLEBY, *he positions the plate whilst* MICKLEBY *back slides the sandwiches. Afterwards,* MICKLEBY *retires with the sandwiches into the hallway.* BLUNDELL *returns to* MABEL.)

BLUNDELL	Have no fear, Mabel. This is Miss Hope, sister of your late Mistress.
MABEL	Oh, streuth!

(BLUNDELL *helps her rise, then he joins* MICKLEBY *out in the hall.*)

HOPE	So it's Mabel, is it?
MABEL	Yes'm.
HOPE	You will wipe that paint from your face, remove that brooch, straighten your hair, and find a clean apron.
MABEL	Come again?
HOPE	Certainly. In future you will wear long sleeves, flat-heeled shoes without buckles or bows, and black woollen stockings.
MABEL	Woollen stockings went out with the bustle.
HOPE	Hold your tongue! If you are dissatisfied . . . resign!
MABEL	But even Miss Faith . . .
HOPE	I am Miss Hope. Now to your duties!
MABEL	Oh Lor! (*Exits* L *in a daze.*)

(HOPE *moves* UR *to the first step of the staircase.*
MICKLEBY *and* BLUNDELL *return into the room.*)

HOPE   These people have stolen my inheritance, but
        they shall not steal my heart nor my home.

MICKLEBY   There *is* a slight complication ...

BLUNDELL   (*quickly*) Whatever you say, Madam.

HOPE   And now I shall spend awhile in
        contemplation. (*Hand to her brow ethereally.*) I
        desire to contact my sister. (*Exits upstairs.*)

BLUNDELL   Going to blow her up on that trumpet.
            Hmmm. So that's her plan — make it so
            miserable for the employees, they'll resign
            and lose their legacies.

        (MICKLEBY *moves down to the sofa, and sits with
        the plate of sandwiches.*)

MICKLEBY   If you hadn't stopped me, I'd've put her
            straight. (*Takes a sandwich.*) How can she dare
            be unpleasant? The Will says she can't fire
            them.

BLUNDELL   (*moving to the sofa*) Yes. The servant is the
            master, the master the servant. But nobody
            has realised, and I don't want 'em to, yet.
            That is a ferocious woman, Mickleby.

        (*He slaps* MICKLEBY'S *shoulder.* MICKLEBY'S
        sandwich flies upwards. BLUNDELL *catches it.*)

        Where did she come from so suddenly?

MICKLEBY   She heard a trumpet.

BLUNDELL   Ectoplasmic twaddle.

MICKLEBY   Oh, was it a twaddle? I thought it was a
            twumpet. Ha ha. Personally, I'm feeling a
            little happier.

        (MICKLEBY *raises a sandwich to his lips.*)

BLUNDELL	I still say it was poison.
	(*Both men arrest their sandwich in mid-bite.*)
MICKLEBY	There goes my appetite.
	(*They drop their sandwiches on the plate and* MICKLEBY *pushes the plate under the sofa.*)
BLUNDELL	I wouldn't mind betting the old man was poisoned, as well.
MICKLEBY	I wonder where they've buried the butler?
BLUNDELL	Yes! Hope murdered the old man and Faith found out so she polished her off, too! Where's the bell.
	(*Moving* R, *he rings the service bell.*)
MICKLEBY	(*to the armchair*) The Doctor said it was ticker trouble.
BLUNDELL	Then he's in it as well.
	(MICKLEBY *groans and flops into the armchair.*)
	Better still – it's some poison which gives the appearance of heart-failure. He's such an old humbug he'd never know.
MICKLEBY	But why should they steal the body?
BLUNDELL	Long term policy: no body, no proof! (*Sits on the arm of the armchair.*)
MABEL	(*entering, moving* C) Yes, sir?
BLUNDELL	Mabel, how long was Mr Barraclough's ah, coffin in the study?
MABEL	All the time sir. Rest his soul.
	(MABEL *does one of her little bobs.* MICKLEBY *half rises and bobs, too.*)
BLUNDELL	Was there anyone with him, at all?
MABEL	Oh yes, sir. Miss Faith hardly left his side from the moment he died. Rest his soul. (*Bobs.*)

(MICKLEBY *rises and bobs.* BLUNDELL *glances at him impatiently.*)

BLUNDELL   What kind of person was he?

MABEL   Oh, lovely, sir.

(*She pauses.* MICKLEBY *leans forward expectantly, then relaxes.*)

Rest his soul.

(MICKLEBY *leaps to his feet.* BLUNDELL *rams him back in the chair.*)

BLUNDELL   Stop fidgeting!

MABEL   And d'you know what his favourite game was, sir, and him almost ninety?

BLUNDELL   No! The old devil!

MABEL   Oh no, sir! Nothing like that!

(*The men's faces drop disappointedly.*)

MICKLEBY   (*under his breath*) Rest his soul.

MABEL   Hide and seek, it was.

BLUNDELL   Aha! Hide and seek.

MABEL   He was always saying "Mabel, hide your eyes". 'Course, I used to kid him on, but every time I opened them, he'd gone! Gave a funny little cackle and disappeared.

BLUNDELL   Did he ever disappear in this room?

MABEL   Everywhere, sir. Upstairs, downstairs, in my lady's chamber.

MICKLEBY   Sounds a bit potty!

BLUNDELL   Thank you very much, my dear. (*Rising, he moves and studies the desk.*)

MABEL   S'alright, sir. Oh, there *was* something you could do for *me*, sir.

MICKLEBY   (*rises, moves to her*) I'll do it, Mabel.

MABEL	Well, sir: all my life people've been giving me tips.
MICKLEBY	Oh, I'm so sorry. (*Fishes in his pocket.*)
MABEL	Oh no! I didn't mean it like that. Honest. It's just that, well, now *I'm* rich, I'd like to see how it feels. Would you mind, sir?
MICKLEBY	Only too willing, Madam. (*He bows and touches his 'cap'.*)
MABEL	Good. (*She fishes a coin from her apron.*) Here's a shilling for your trouble. (*Airily she drops it into* MICKLEBY's *palm.*)
MICKLEBY	Thank you, M'am. Thank you.
MABEL	Don't mention it I'm sure. (*She flounces to the kitchen door.*) Oh, you'll give 'im half, won't you. (*Exits.*)
	(BLUNDELL *joins* MICKLEBY. MICKLEBY, *with a jaunty laugh, throws up the coin and tries to catch it over his shoulder. But* BLUNDELL *catches it instead. He pockets it.*)
MICKLEBY	Ooooogh!
BLUNDELL	'Teach you not to throw your money about. Now, help me find this secret panel.
MICKLEBY	Right you are. (*To stairs, then stops.*) Which secret panel?
BLUNDELL	How else could old Barraclough disappear, dead *or* alive? (*Slaps his fist.*) And why didn't Mabel peep through her fingers?
MICKLEBY	You can't suspect Mabel?
BLUNDELL	Young. Strong. She could help carry a body.
MICKLEBY	Look out! Here's Buffalo Bill.
DOCTOR	(*enters* R, *jacket over his arm*) Is any peoples here? (*He crosses to Caesar's bust.*)

BLUNDELL   Hubert, we shall put the cat among the
            beneficiaries.

DOCTOR   (*to the bust*) Ah, nossink more to be done.
            Later, the necessary document I am signink.

BLUNDELL   Doctor! I believe murder has been done.

            (MICKLEBY *groans and exits into the hall.*)

DOCTOR   (*to the bust*) Beg to pardon?

BLUNDELL   (*shouts*) Miss Faith was poisoned.

DOCTOR   Gut gut gut. (*He proceeds up the stairs, then
            turns.*) Excuse please, 'Poisoned' am you
            sayink?

BLUNDELL   (*to bottom step*) Poisoned, yes.

            (*Unseen, the bookcase panel slides open: hidden
            ears are listening in the dark recess. Slowly it closes
            again.*)

DOCTOR   Poisoned, am she? Himmel tush tush! A
            tinge about the lips I am noticink. Most
            exciting. Again I shall examine the younk
            lady, directly I am havink my wash and
            brush. Thenk you, Doktor. (*Exits upstairs.*)

MICKLEBY   (*hurries in*) There's hearse drawn up. A
            hearse outside.

BLUNDELL   Damn, I'd forgotten the Undertaker. Wonder
            how much he knows?

MICKLEBY   D'you think he's the murderer?

BLUNDELL   Why should the undertaker be a murderer?

MICKLEBY   (*shrugs*) Good for business.

            (MR SORRELL *enters. His face has a green and
            tacitrun atmosphere of frozen grief. all else is
            black: black tail coat, black top hat, black gloves,
            black everything. He stands between the solicitors.
            They react appropriately.*)

SORRELL	I am Mr Sorrell, Mortician and Monumental Mason.
BLUNDELL	I am Mr Blundell, Solicitor and Commissioner for Oaths.
MICKLEBY	I'm worried.
BLUNDELL	How do you do, Mr Sorrell.
SORRELL	Wretched fibrositis all down my neck.
BLUNDELL	Well, maybe when the weather clears.
SORRELL	It won't. That bridge'll down within the hour. Things have been sort of messed-up at the Parlour ... what with the twins, followed by the floods.
MICKLEBY	Who'd be a father.
BLUNDELL	I don't see any of your men, Mr Sorrell.
SORRELL	Didn't bring any. Perhaps you gentlemen would take an end each?
MICKLEBY	How did I guess?
SORRELL	It's our best model, you know. Solid brass handles. Shame to have it up here. Mr Barraclough'd've looked lovely at the shop. We have our own private mortuary.
MICKLEBY	Oh you live on the premises?
SORRELL	I have a couple of brochures with me. Perhaps you'd care to take one home. Distance no object. (*Deftly producing two brochures from an inside pocket, he hands them one each.*)
BLUNDELL	Thank you.
MICKLEBY	Yes, when I'm thinking of going down, I'll look you up.
SORRELL	Is Mr Barraclough still in the study?
BLUNDELL	More or less.

SORRELL   Ah well, I'd better be screwing him down.

MICKLEBY   Expecting a struggle?

SORRELL   For the Happy Journey.

MICKLEBY   No offence. (*He coughs.*)

SORRELL   Was that a cough, sir?

MICKLEBY   No. (*Shocked, he backs to the sofa.*) No, no,
              thank you.

              (SORRELL *is a tenacious salesman. He follows
              swiftly.* MICKLEBY *sits defensively.*)

              It was just a frog in my throat. Lively little
              thing.

              (BLUNDELL *moves above the sofa and leans over.*
              SORRELL *is at the* R *end.* MICKLEBY *is oppressed
              by their pessimistic faces. He has a dreadful desire
              to cough and tries hard to stifle the urge, but
              eventually and involuntarily gives way to a loud
              splutter. He flops full length on the sofa.* SORRELL
              whips out expanding metal rule.)

SORRELL   Watch it, sir. My laugh is always the last.
              (*Moves towards the study.*)

              (*Unobtrusively,* BLUNDELL *has brought a lily from
              the bowl* UR. *Now he places it on* MICKLEBY'S
              *chest, then he moves and solemnly draws the
              archway curtains.*)

BLUNDELL   Mr Sorrell. I fear there is someone else in the
              study. Miss Faith died this afternoon.

              (*The dog howls off.*)

SORRELL   Oh how sad ... in a manner of speaking.
              (*Whips out a little book.*) Let me see, about five
              feet six, I believe. ... Is there no member of
              the family here?

BLUNDELL   Miss Hope Barraclough is upstairs.

SORRELL   Yes. Yes, she would be.

BLUNDELL	(*into his ear*) Do you know what she looks like? Or anything about the lady?

(HOPE *appears on the stairs followed by* ANNE.)

SORRELL	I never discuss people. Causes scandal and tragedy. Don't mind tragedy, can't bear scandal.
HOPE	My sentiments entirely.

(HOPE *sweeps downstairs to* RC. BLUNDELL *breaks to* LC *and* MICKLEBY *joins him, placing the lily on the chest.*)

SORRELL	"De mortuis Nil Nisi Bonum" as we say in the Trade ... My sincere condolences Madam and I trust I may have the honour of attending your late sister.
HOPE	A long time since we met, Mr Sorrell.
SORRELL	Minutes, days, years. In my business we just wait. They all come in the end. (*Exits.*)

(*The great bell cl-a-a-angs above. Lightning and thunder.* JOHNSON *enters* C. *He has been in the rain. His hair is dishevelled and his tunic is unbuttoned.*)

JOHNSON	The bridge, Madam! The bridge is down.
BLUNDELL MICKLEBY	} (*together*) The bridge! (*They rush out.*)

(HOPE *turns to face* JOHNSON. *He is startled, and takes a tentative step towards her.*)

JOHNSON	But you are ... !
HOPE	Is it quite impossible to cross?
JOHNSON	'Fraid so.
HOPE	And is that the way you dress in my house?
JOHNSON	I've been in the storm, Missy.

HOPE	In my service you dress properly at all times.
JOHNSON	What am I, dirt or something?
HOPE	If my attitude offends you ... resign!
JOHNSON	Talk about peas in a pod. (*Exits* L.)
	(HOPE *moves to the stairs.* BLUNDELL *and* MICKLEBY *return, collars up-turned.*)
BLUNDELL	Miss Barraclough, we're marooned.
HOPE	And likely to be so for some while.
MICKLEBY	Oh no.
HOPE	I like the idea even less than you, Mr Mickleby, but ... (*Sinisterly.*) make yourself at home. (*She exits upstairs.*)
MICKLEBY	Must think we live at the Rue de Morgue.
SORRELL	(*enters* R) I thought you said Miss Faith was in here.
BLUNDELL MICKLEBY	(*together*) She is.
SORRELL	She's not.
BLUNDELL MICKLEBY	(*together*) What?
	(*Lightning and* thunder. BLUNDELL *dashes into the study.* MICKLEBY *rushes to the telephone.*)
MICKLEBY	(*into the phone*) Help! ... Help!
	(*Lightning and* thunder. BLUNDELL *hurries back to* MICKLEBY.)
BLUNDELL	She's vanished. Gone.
MICKLEBY	But not forgotten. (*Into phone.*) Hello? ... Oh hell!
	(*The flex dangles raggedly. He passes the instrument to* BLUNDELL.)
	Dead, Uncle. It's dead.
BLUNDELL	It's all yours.
	(*He hands it to the Undertaker.*)

CURTAIN

(Music to interval)

ACT TWO
Scene One

Ten Minutes Later.

HOPE *is sitting in her armchair.* BLUNDELL *enters from the study,
jacket collar turned up. He carries a torch.*

BLUNDELL   She couldn't have been taken that way.
            Plenty of mud outside the study windows. No
            footprints.

HOPE   There are those who cast neither shadows
            nor footprints.

BLUNDELL   I do wish you would consider my idea, Miss
            Barraclough.

HOPE   There are no secret panels in my house, Mr
            Blundell.

BLUNDELL   But there is no other way she could have
            been spirited from that room.

HOPE   You have yourself given the
            solution —— in the word 'spirited'.

            (*There is a loud clatter as* MICKLEBY *half
            stumbles, half slithers down the stairs, frightened to
            death. On seeing them, he assumes a casual air.*)

BLUNDELL   What is it?

MICKLEBY   Nothing up there. (*Rubbing a suave eyebrow, he
            saunters 'Bond style' to sit on the edge of the sofa.*)

HOPE   They will not find her.

BLUNDELL   With respect, Madam, we cannot just dismiss
            this as 'dematerialisation'.

HOPE   (*rising, moving to the stairs*) As soon as the
            bridge is repaired ... we shall inform the
            police.

BLUNDELL   It may be too late by then.

HOPE   (*pauses on the stairs*) Too late for what?

BLUNDELL	I asked Dr Brown to re-examine your sister for signs of poison.
HOPE	(*ominously*) Indeed?
BLUNDELL	And I believe her body has been stolen to prevent that examination.
HOPE	(*raging*) I am sick and tired of your pathetic theories, and of your interference in the affairs of my family.
BLUNDELL	Even if a crime has been committed?
HOPE	A crime! That is laughable coming from you, after your criminal mis-use of my father's Will. Don't overtry my patience, you vile man. (*She exits upstairs.*)

(*The dog howls outside.*)

BLUNDELL	(*to the dog*) Oh shut up! (*Mops his brow.*) I've a feeling we lost that round.
MICKLEBY	(*rises, moves to the armchair*) Yes. 'Vile' was a bit uncharitable. I'd've settled for 'nosy'. You do lean to the nosy, y'know, sir.
BLUNDELL	Because I believe in the long arm of the Law. Ooogh, how I'd love to fling that dummy arm at her feet and say "Shake hands with your Dad, kid!"

(*He flops into the armchair. A second later he rises and strides across the room.*)

Come on, we're wasting time. Check these walls again. Buttons, springs, anything. Look inside that armour.

MICKLEBY	Where are you off to?
BLUNDELL	The kitchen. Going to look through the Cook's drawers. (*Exits.*)

(*Moving cautiously to the armour, MICKLEBY peeps under the headpiece. He blows into it, and coughs through a cloud of dust. Next he taps a panel.)*

MICKLEBY   If anyone tapped back, I'd die.

(MICKLEBY *creeps to the oak chest. He lifts the lid (to an eerie creaking), shouts hoarsly and drops it with a bang.)*

Empty!

(As he creeps to the panels BC, SORRELL *silently appears on the stairs above him.* MICKLEBY *taps a panel. He taps again. And* SORRELL, *mystified, taps back.* MICKLEBY *is mortified. Then he looks upwards.)*

Oh, it's you.

SORRELL   (*descending*) Why were you tapping the panels?

MICKLEBY   Just playing with the woodworm . . . Any sign of the missing bodies?

SORRELL   No-o-ogh. Not so much as a single tooth.

MICKLEBY   Brrr . . .

SORRELL   That was a shiver. Not coming down with anything, are we?

MICKLEBY   We? Who's your undertaker?

SORRELL   Mmmm . . . (*Circling him, doubtfully.*) You never can tell. I did a man on Tuesday.

MICKLEBY   Good Lord.

SORRELL   Only a week previously I'd seen him looking much as you do now.

MICKLEBY   I'm a little tired. I've been breathing all day.

SORRELL   Strangely enough that is what *he* said. "I'm a little tired", he said. The Poof! There he was in one of our oak specials. (*He spreads his hands, illustrating a sarcophagus.*)

MICKLEBY   You're dead keen on advertising, aren't you!

SORRELL   Ah.

MICKLEBY   You ought to carry a placard saying
               "Eventually – Why Not Now?"

SORRELL   I do not comprehend, sir.

MICKLEBY   It was a joke. Do you never succumb to a
               giggle?

SORRELL   Laughing makes you fat. Fat undertakers are
               frowned upon.

               (*He walks slowly towards the kitchen.* MICKLEBY
               falls in behind 'Dead March' fashion. SORRELL
               turns at the door.)

               I am somewhat peckish. I wonder if
               sustenance has been provided?

MICKLEBY   I understand there's somthing cold laid out
               in the kitchen.

               (*Both exit gloomily.* HOPE *appears on the stairs,
               followed by* ANNE.)

HOPE   Ah, the shadows! They are my friends. I'm
               sometimes hypnotised by their mystery and
               share awhile the tortures, the pleasures of
               these obscene dancing goblins. (*She lays her
               shawl on one end of the sofa and sits on the other
               end.*) Do you Believe, Miss Beale? In
               Spiritualism?

ANNE   I've never given it much thought.

HOPE   Oh you should – it's most revealing. For
               instance, I have discovered something about
               my sister.

ANNE   I am innocent of her death, Miss Hope.

HOPE   Oh, that stupid accusation! No, no, this is an
               affair concerning … Come in, Mr Johnson!

               (JOHNSON *parts the curtains with a swish.* HOPE,
               as did FAITH, *speaks without looking at him.*)

This old house has such big ears.

JOHNSON   Anything that concerns my fiancee concerns me.

(ANNE *joins him at* C.)

HOPE   Two love birds with one stone.

JOHNSON   You what?

HOPE   A moment ago, in my sister's room, a friendly spirit *guided* me to a certain drawer. In this drawer I discovered a most interesting document.

(ANNE *gasps, placing a hand on* JOHNSON'S *arm.*)

It referred to a diamond necklace, our prized heirloom. Your bride-to-be apparently stole it.

ANNE   No!

HOPE   But the paper I found is a confession written by you.

JOHNSON   Listen, Miss Barraclough, I can explain.

HOPE   (*interrupting*) I'm asking your fiancee, if you please.

JOHNSON   But I can explain just as easy.

HOPE   (*shouts*) Will you be quiet! Your fiancee will plead her own case, thank you. (HOPE *rises and crosses to the desk.*) Were you a thief, Miss Beale?

ANNE   Only for the moment. I'd have replaced it but she wouldn't let me.

HOPE   She?

ANNE   Your sister. It was an impulse.

HOPE	Dear me, it is involved, my child. (*She takes an envelope from the little chest.*) Tell me the extenuating circumstances. I'm sure they're numerous.
ANNE	Oh Ted, what's the use. (ANNE *moves round and sits on the sofa.*)
HOPE	A great deal of use to me. It's my necklace.
	(*She brings a pen, ink bottle, blotting and the envelope, and sits in the armchair. Then she addresses the envelope on the small table next to the armchair.*)
	Come along! When did all this happen?
ANNE	It was a Thursday, two months ago. Miss Faith called me into the study and asked me to open the safe for her. She had sprained her wrist gardening.
HOPE	(*quickly*) How did you know the combination?
ANNE	Miss Faith dictated the numbers.
HOPE	My father kept them a secret. How could Faith have known?
JOHNSON	How could Anne have known?
HOPE	(*triumphantly*) She was his secretary.
JOHNSON	Go on, dear.
ANNE	She merely looked inside, told me to close it and left me alone in the room. (*Whispers.*) I saw the necklace. All those diamonds. Sparkling. And so beautiful.
HOPE	M'yes, we liked it, too. (*She removes a hair from the pen-knib.*)
ANNE	I only meant to touch it. Touch it ... but on the spur of the moment, I fastened the clasp around my neck. Just to wear it for a second. I swear.

HOPE	(*growls to herself*) Pity. Pity; all so sorry for themselves.
ANNE	Then I leaned back and accidentally closed the door of the safe. It was horrible. I couldn't open it. And ... oh I know *now*, but I panicked. And at that very moment, Miss Faith came in and saw me.
JOHNSON	She didn't give her a chance to explain.
ANNE	I was *made* to write that confession. She said, "I'll put you on probation."
JOHNSON	(*moves in to* HOPE) For probation read blackmail.
HOPE	Oh, be logical! My sister had nothing to gain.
JOHNSON	(*fiercly*) Except power! And she loved that. She liked to play God and have people jump when she pulled the string. Anne's life was a misery with that confession waved in her face. Your sister was rotten. Rotten!
HOPE	(*rising*) Enough! Finish! You will not insult or browbeat *me*! Keep your place!
	(JOHNSON *swings away to near the panel.* ANNE *remains seated.* MICKLEBY *enters* L, *still tapping the walls.*)
MICKLEBY	Oh, excuse me. Just knocking around. Ha ha. (*He moves towards the hall, then freezes when an owl hoots outside.*) Good gracious! That was no dog.
HOPE	It was an owl.
MICKLEBY	I know, but who's howling? (*He exits* C.)
HOPE	(*replacing the ink bottle, etc. on the desk*) The evidence was circumstantial. Only a fool would write such a confession.
JOHNSON	Anne's brother is in prison for theft!
ANNE	(*rises*) Ted, please!

JOHNSON	(*moving above the armchair*) Your sister's word against Anne's – who'd they believe? A thief for a brother, finger-prints on the safe and she was caught hiding the . . . the 'swag'.
HOPE	Hmm, yes. Yes, it might almost be true.
JOHNSON	And so?
	(HOPE *crosses over and picks up her shawl from the sofa.*)
	What're you going to do, Miss Barraclough?
HOPE	There is only one thing I can do. (*A pause, whilst she moves to her armchair and sits.*) I must tear up that confession.
	(ANNE *and* TED *move together, hardly believing their ears.*)
ANNE	Miss Barraclough, I could never thank you enough.
HOPE	I think you could.
JOHNSON	Why?
HOPE	This affair will always be an embarrassment to us. You will both hand in your resignations, and leave as soon as the bridge is repaired.
ANNE	But . . . but Ted would lose his legacy.
HOPE	I'm so sorry.
ANNE	But that isn't fair. Me, yes. But why should Ted?
HOPE	When you are married it will be share and share alike. You may as well start now.
JOHNSON	Congratulations. Faith'd have been proud of you.
HOPE	(*quickly, viciously*) Save your insults until after the confession is destroyed. That will be all.

JOHNSON	Not quite! (*In a swift movement, he grabs the envelope off the table.*)
HOPE	The envelope is empty as yet. Though you will notice I've labelled it 'Evidence For The Police' in readiness.
	(JOHNSON *throws down the envelope and draws the revolver he found in Act One, threatening* HOPE *across the table.*)
JOHNSON	All right, where is it?
	[N.B. *The following lines are played at great speed, overlapping and building to a crescendo.*]
ANNE	No, Ted, no!
JOHNSON	She's playing her sister's game.
ANNE	You can't do it!
JOHNSON	I'll try anything once.
ANNE	No!
JOHNSON	Yes, anything!
	(JOHNSON *pushes* ANNE *aside. She backs away, thoroughly scared.*)
HOPE	Aren't we being rather foolhardy?
JOHNSON	Three seconds, Miss Barraclough. (*He points the gun to her head.*) I mean it.
HOPE	Why wait? Pull the trigger now. Go on! And we shall know who the killer *really* is.
	(JOHNSON *hesitates for a second. Then he closes his eyes, shakes his head.*)
JOHNSON	(*whispers*) We can't win. We never win.
	(*He lowers the gun and turns to look hopelessly at* ANNE, *who hurries out* L, *with a sob.*)
HOPE	Leave the pistol, if you please!
	(JOHNSON *tosses it on to the sofa. He strides to the doorway* L, *and turns back.*)

JOHNSON   Is Faith really dead? (*Exits.*)

               (HOPE *rises and hurriedly takes a paper from her dress, places it in the envelope, seals the flap and picks up the revolver from the sofa. Next she twists a miniature painting on the back wall. The panel slides open. She hides the paper and gun within and closes the panel.*)

HOPE   Three down and four to go!

               (HOPE *notices a fluttering of the hall curtains. Swiftly she pulls them aside.* MABEL *is standing there.*)

MABEL   I was just straightening the curtains, Mum.

HOPE   You mean you were spying on me. Come here! (*Dragging her into the room.*) What did you see?

MABEL   Nothin', Mum. I've just been dusting the vestibule.

HOPE   What did you see?

               (HOPE *twists* MABEL'S *arm behind her back, forcing the poor girl against the armchair.*)

MABEL   (*screeches*) Nothing, Mum. Nothing.

               (HOPE *releases her, moving above her to the table.*)

HOPE   Look at that table! When did you dust it last?

MABEL   This morning, Mum.

HOPE   You're a liar and slovenly worker. Polish it immediately or you'll do it on your evening off.

               (*Moving to the desk,* HOPE *angrily slams shut the lid of the little chest. In so doing, she knocks the bell to the floor.*)

HOPE   Pick up this bell!

MABEL   Oh gawd!

HOPE	And tell Anne Beale to bring envelopes. I have just used the last one.
	(MABEL *shrinks away.*)
	Pick up the bell!
MABEL	It's all happened before ... the bell, the envelopes. You sound just like Miss Faith.
HOPE	Oh these miserable insignificant mentalities. (*She ascends the stairs.*) You will tell Cook I expect dinner on time to the second. No excuses for floods ... legacies ... or anything else.
	(*Her voice fades into the distance as she exits.* MICKLEBY *yells off* C, *then he rushes into the room and rests panting against the armchair.* MABEL *has moved to pick up the bell.*)
MICKLEBY	Uncle! Uncle! Oh, awful, terrible.
BLUNDELL	(*rushing in*) What's up? What happened?
MICKLEBY	A ghost! I've just seen a ghost in the hall, with a brass head and green hair.
	(BLUNDELL *peers carefully into the hall, then returns.*)
BLUNDELL	Fool! It's an aspidistra.
MABEL	Excuse me, sir. (*Crosses to* BLUNDELL.) Miss Hope just said there weren't any envelopes in that chest.
BLUNDELL	Yes, dear?
MABEL	But this afternoon Miss Faith made Anne fetch a whole bunch of envelopes from the study.
BLUNDELL	Oh yes?
MABEL	Well, I mean, It's so creepy. Miss Faith couldn't possibly've used them all. A whole bunch of envelopes, there were, just before I fed Hector.

MICKLEBY   Hector? Who's he?

MABEL   The late Mr Barraclough's guinea pig. He
            lives in the conservatoire.

MICKLEBY   Oh! Musical!

MABEL   And Miss Faith only gave me one letter to
            post.

BLUNDELL   (*thoughtfully*) I wonder? D'you know when she
            wrote this letter?

MABEL   'Bout quarter to three. In here.

BLUNDELL   Is anyone other than the family allowed to
            use that chest?

MABEL   Oh no, sir. Proper holy ground, that is.

            (ANNE *enters* L, *un-noticed.*)

BLUNDELL   Do you still have the letter she asked you to
            post, Mabel?

MABEL   Ooogh yes. (*She produces it from a pocket in her
            dress.*)

BLUNDELL   Perhaps I'd better keep it, until someone in
            authority arrives.

ANNE   (*quickly*) Mabel! Miss Hope is ringing for you.

MABEL   Oh Streuth!

            (*Just as* BLUNDELL *is about to take the letter,*
            MABEL *runs upstairs with it.*)

BLUNDELL   Miss Beale, would you kindly spare me the
            odd second?

            (MICKLEBY *moves in and grins at* ANNE *over his
            Uncle's shoulder.*)

ANNE   If you wish.

BLUNDELL   Thank you, my dear. (*Then to* MICKLEBY.)
            You want to see the guinea pig, don't you?

MICKLEBY   Guinea pig? Me?

BLUNDELL	Hector. (*Meaningly.*) He's in the conservatoire.
MICKLEBY	Oh, you want to be alone with . . . oh. Naughty old man! (*Exits quickly* C.)
ANNE	(*firmly*) I did not poison the tea, Mr Blundell.
BLUNDELL	I'm sure you didn't – as sure as I am the tea had no connection with her death.
ANNE	Oh, I killed her in some other way?
BLUNDELL	My dear young lady, I am not a policeman. (*With great charm,* BLUNDELL *takes her arm and leads her on a ramble around the room.*) . . . Merely a dull old solicitor seeking light in ah, strange circumstances. (*Pats her hand.*) You know this six month Clause in the Will creates a unique situation.
ANNE	I'm sure Miss Hope will find an answer.
BLUNDELL	No. You see, she is legally bound to keep you in employment. She cannot dismiss you. If you wished, therefore, you needn't work at all.
ANNE	(*ruefully*) It's like winning a holiday cruise in prison.
BLUNDELL	It is? Still, you needn't be worried if she is tempted to ah, force your resignation, eh? Ha ha.
ANNE	(*frowns to herself*) Thank you.
BLUNDELL	On the other hand I'm rather anxious – do sit down, dear. (*Having meandered round to below the sofa,* ANNE *sits on it.* BLUNDELL *joins her.*) Rather anxious we don't tell the others yet! A domestic uprising'd be more than I could handle at the moment.
ANNE	I can certainly speak for Mr Johnson and myself.

BLUNDELL	Good. Forgive my asking but ah, is he your young man?
ANNE	We are engaged.
BLUNDELL	Oh splendid! Ha ha! Jolly good. Tell me, why did the sisters adopt their stepfather's name?
ANNE	I believe they preferred it to their own.
BLUNDELL	Ah! Now you may think me quite cuckoo, Miss Beale, but was their own name . . . don't laugh, will you! . . . Nikkamoppaloffkis?
ANNE	No. It was Shufflebottom.
BLUNDELL	Oh. Well, we all have our troubles. (*Rising* BLUNDELL *moves up to* C *and, his back to* ANNE, *surveys the walls.*) When I searched the house just now, I couldn't find any cellars. Is that not strange in a building of this age?
ANNE	They . . . they were blocked up many years ago. The old well caused dampness.
BLUNDELL	(*swings round*) There's an old well under this house?
ANNE	Yes. The villagers say it's an ancient Druid's well. There was some legend that anything dropped into it would disappear forever.
	(*The study door closes suddenly, with a long creak and a bang!*)
BLUNDELL	Really? (*He shivers.*) Then were it still in existence – with a secret entrance? After all, bodies must go somewhere.
ANNE	Oh no, that's too horrible.
BLUNDELL	As Mr Barraclough's secretary, were you acquainted with the terms of his Will?
	(BLUNDELL *grows more and more forceful, quickly snapping his questions as in a court room.*

The scene builds to a climax, with ANNE *becoming more and more agitated.*)

BLUNDELL   Miss Beale?

ANNE   Yes.

BLUNDELL   (*behind her, speaking above her*) Then you noticed we read the wrong Will! Yes, Miss Beale?

ANNE   Yes.

BLUNDELL   And yet you made no mention.

ANNE   (*rising*) I assumed you had some reason. Besides, I was too upset.

BLUNDELL   (*follows*) Upset? Before Miss Faith grew sick? (*Speaking across the armchair.*) *Before* she accused you?

ANNE   No. I meant . . . .

BLUNDELL   Ted Johnson knew the terms of the Will, didn't he? Being your fiance, your told him.

ANNE   (*swings round*) What are you suggesting?

BLUNDELL   That you are frightened, Miss Beale. You've been frightened ever since Mr Barraclough died – because Ted Johnson killed him for the legacy.

ANNE   No!

BLUNDELL   Then murdered Faith because she found out.

ANNE   It's untrue! Ted's never done anything.

BLUNDELL   Then why did Faith accuse *you*? What was the reason.

ANNE   Nothing. Nothing. Nothing! It's over. Finished.

BLUNDELL   Finished? What? Blackmail?

ANNE   No! (*She hurries upstairs.*)

BLUNDELL   (*moving up to her*) I'm only trying to help.

ANNE (*spiritedly*) The best way you can help is by leaving us alone. Your bumbling and meddling are useless! Useless!

BLUNDELL I'm sorry, but one more impersonal question, Miss Beale. (*To the foot of the stairs.*) The last one, I promise.

(MICKLEBY *enters* C.)

MICKLEBY You and that perishing guinea pig! I said: "Hello! Chuck chuck chuck!" Flipping animal bit me finger!

(*He draws his left hand from his jacket, revealing a globular bandage on his index finger.*)

BLUNDELL Sssssh! (*To* ANNE.) Could you tell us the name of this missing beneficiary?

ANNE There were two missing beneficiaries.

MICKLEBY *Two?*

ANNE One was Dr Brown.

MICKLEBY Dr Brown, yes.

ANNE And the other was an actor friend of Mr Barraclough's. I think his real name was Popkiss on the stage . . . .

BLUNDELL Actor! What was his full name, dear?

ANNE Nicholas M. Pope or Popkiss.

BLUNDELL
MICKLEBY } (*shaking hands, together*) Nikkamoppalloffkis!

BLUNDELL At last! What does he do on the stage?

ANNE I believe it's some kind of female impersonation act.

MICKLEBY Ever met the chap?

ANNE He's only been here once in my time.

BLUNDELL What did he look like? (*Mounting two stairs.*)

ANNE	Oh, he was an ordinary man. Clean shaven. Medium height. I saw him at a distance.
BLUNDELL	Thank you very much, Miss Beale. And once again, I'm sorry.
ANNE	(*sternly*) So am I! (*Exits upstairs.*)
	(BLUNDELL *comes down from the stairs, slaps a jovial arm around* MICKLEBY, *and leads him round below the staircase.*)
BLUNDELL	Hubert dear boy, there is a glimmer of hope!
MICKLEBY	As long as it's not Faith – she's dead. . . . Female impersonator. You don't suppose the Cook is Nikkamoppaloffkis – in a wig and a couple of pomegranates?
	(MABEL *enters from upstairs, sniffing tearfully.*)
MABEL	Here's that letter, sir.
	(*Passing the letter over the banisters to* BLUNDELL, MABEL *descends. She moves to the sofa, dabbing her nose with a hanky.*)
BLUNDELL	Thank you, Mabel.
	(BLUNDELL *sits in the armchair, examining the envelope.* MICKLEBY *follows* MABEL.)
MICKLEBY	Something the matter, dear?
MABEL	Everyth-th-thing. She's been at me again and I'm proper f-f-ed up . . . . . (*With a howl, she bursts into tears, sitting on the sofa.*)
MICKLEBY BLUNDELL	} (*together*) Aw . . . !
MICKLEBY	(*sitting beside* MABEL) Waddems matter then, dear. Mmmm?
MABEL	It's her . . . Miss Hope . . . keeps seeing dust everywhere. Must have magnifying eyeballs.
BLUNDELL	Don't you take any notice.

MABEL	She says my wages'll suffer.
MICKLEBY	Humbug! She can't touch your wages.
MABEL	She can't?
MICKLEBY	Good Lord no!
BLUNDELL	(*warningly*) Mickleby!
MICKLEBY	The old boy said so, Uncle. "Board and keep as up the time of my death".
MABEL	Can't she fire us, either?
MICKLEBY	(*shouts merrily*) No-o-ogh!
BLUNDELL	(*to himself*) No-o-ogh! (*Slaps his head exasperatedly.*)
MABEL	'Ere, what'd she do if we didn't work at all, then?
MICKLEBY	(*expansively*) Nothing. Ha ha!
BLUNDELL	(*imitating him again*) Nothing ho ho!
MABEL	So we're not flippin' servants at all!
MICKLEBY	No – ha ha. Come to think of it, you're flippin' share-holders.
MABEL	Whoopee!

(*She grabs* MICKLEBY, *tugging him on to her lap. She gives him a whopping kiss, then rises, depositing him on the floor.*)

BLUNDELL	(*rising*) Where're you going, dear?

(*Removing her apron,* MABEL *tosses it over her shoulder and, with hips a-swinging, flounces to the hall opening.*)

MABEL	If h'anybody wants me, I shall be in the Blue Room.

(*She exits, like Cleopatra into the temple.* BLUNDELL *picks up the apron. He kneels on the sofa – overlooking* MICKLEBY – *who is still sprawled on the floor, happily licking his lips.*)

BLUNDELL   Finished your lunch?

MICKLEBY   Eh?

BLUNDELL   (*flings the apron at him*) Wipe the jam off your
            face! One foot in hell, and you start a blasted
            revolution. (*Moves to the hall.*) I'm going to
            soak this envelope in the washroom.

            (MICKLEBY *rises and follows up to the hallway
            opening.*)

MICKLEBY   Why?

BLUNDELL   Chemistry, Mickleby. And beware.
            (*Dramatically.*) Because if this envelope turns
            black, it will have been poisoned by someone
            behind these walls. (*Exits.*)

MICKLEBY   Poor old Uncle. Gone off his bonce.

DOCTOR   (*entering* L) Are anybody here?

MICKLEBY   Only us chickens!

DOCTOR   Ah! Younk lady!

MICKLEBY   Male, sir, actually.

DOCTOR   (*peering at* MICKLEBY'S *chest*) Ach, so it are.

            (DR BROWN *is standing in front of the panel.*
            MICKLEBY *is beside him.*)

            The missink bodies, is they yet findink them?

MICKLEBY   'Fraid not, sir.

DOCTOR   Hm. Under all the beds I are searchinks.
            There are nothinks!

MICKLEBY   Mm, everythink's missink in this house.

            (MICKLEBY *now concentrates on a stain on his
            sleeve. He licks a hanky and rubs.*)

            Doctor – hate talking shop, but I'm worried
            over Mr Blundell. Frankly, this trouble has
            unsettled him.

Understandable in this house: even the
beetles are death watch. And ... you
know ... stitch in time ...

(*During all this, the panel slide open, a Hooded
Figure claps its hand over* DR BROWN'S *mouth
and drags him into the recess. The panel closes.*)

I thought if you had the odd aspirin or
something. (*He turns round ... and runs up the
stairs in terror.*)
Uncle! ... Uncle! ... UNCLE!!!

CURTAIN

ACT TWO
Scene Two

Five Minutes Later.

MABEL *reclines on the sofa in all her glad rags, flourishing an
exotic drink in a long-stemmed cocktail glass.* AGNES *is pacing
uneasily in Cook's attire with a flowery hat.*

MABEL	Now this is what I call living.
AGNES	I call it trouble
MABEL	(*sets her glass on the chest*) We're shareholders in this establishment, aren't we?
AGNES	I feel out of place I'm going back to 'kitchen.
	(MABEL *rises upstage and stops her.*)
MABEL	Hasn't she brought it on herself, being nasty and ranting and raving?
AGNES	Ee, I feel peculiar ... Mr Barraclough and Miss Faith all dead in there.
MABEL	I'll tell you a secret ... the old boy's just sandbags and Faith is thin air.
AGNES	Eee, give over! Bodies all snatched?
MABEL	Yes. And my stomach's still itching, so we haven't finished with death even yet.

AGNES   Ee, it's enough to sink me fruit cake.

MABEL   Well, there's nothing wrong sitting next to sandbags, is there. (*She retrieves her cocktail and sits on the sofa.*)

AGNES   I should be checking that roast.

MABEL   Oh let it smoulder.

AGNES   What else do you know, love?

(*We grow suspicious of* AGNES. *She moves behind* MABEL, *and there seems a sinister touch to her question.*)

And what sort of poison was it all?

MABEL   Come on, assie-vooze on the chezzy-long with Mabel.

AGNES   (*sits*) I daresay you get used to bodies. I sometimes look at a leg o'lamb or a pig's head in the larder.

MABEL   Look at Miss Hope upstairs. She's got evil eyes —— in both her heads.

(HOPE *appears on the stairs, carrying her shawl. She remains quite still and listens.*)

AGNES   But she wouldn't harm her own sister.

MABEL   Wouldn't she just! It strikes me as funny that as soon as Faith pops off, up pops Hope! You mark my words, Aggie! If Hope disappears, keep your eyes peeled – cos any time at all, Charity'll pop along.

(HOPE *now glides down the stairs and round to the armchair.*)

MABEL   It's a bloomin' funny family.

HOPE   You find us amusing?

(*Both women leap to their feet with a yelp.* HOPE *places her shawl on the armchair.* MABEL *assumes a brave but jerky flippancy.*)

MABEL	Well, if it isn't the Duchess!
HOPE	Obviously there is some explanation for this exhibition?
MABEL	Nope. I just felt like a quiet h'aperitoff in the lounge, don't you know. (*She sits down, airily popping the cherry into her mouth.*)
HOPE	And you, Cook? Are you not drinking?
AGNES	No. Wine and stuff is poison to me. (*Faux pas.*) Poison, ee'eck! (*Urgently.*) Let's get back, Mabel.
MABEL	No fear! (*To* HOPE.) If you must know, Duchess, I've called a strike. So if you want the beds made or the dusting done . . . get at it yourself!
HOPE	(*seething*) I may be forced to employ you, but I'm not standing for this. You'll work, Mabel, and you'll work as you've never worked before.
MABEL	Will I? And if I refuse?
HOPE	You can't refuse —. (*She stops, realising.*)
MABEL	Yes, you can't do a thing. The lawyer said so. There's a bob, Duchess. Buy yourself an aspirin. (MABEL *produces a coin and drops it airily at* HOPE's *feet.*)
HOPE	I see. (*To* AGNES.) Are these also your sentiments?
MABEL	Don't let her bully you, Agnes.
HOPE	She'll speak for herself.
AGNES	Well, Mum, I know nothing of strikes. But what Mabel's getting at is . . . even though we're servants, we still have hopes'n dreams'n pride. D'you follow? Secretly, me and Mabel think we're quite posh' in our own little way. I mean, we treat you like a lady. Can't you just pretend a bit of respect in return?

HOPE	Respect? You worm youselves into my money, and demand respect.
AGNES	Aye, it's been rankling, hasn't it. I can understand. Seven thousand pounds! I'd never dreamt so much could be mine. But . . . . (*Holding back the tears.*) . . . but if it means that much to you, I don't want it!
MABEL	(*rising*) Aggie, don't!
AGNES	No, love. I've never had nowt I didn't work for, and I'm happy to go on 'same. Keep your money, Miss Barraclough. Tomorrow I'll be on me way.
MABEL	No, Aggie!
HOPE	I am to accept this as your resignation, then?
MABEL	Not on your bustle!
AGNES	No, Mabel. I've had me say.
	(AGNES *moves behind* MABEL *and stands, facing upstage, near the panel.*)
MABEL	Well I haven't! What! – stand by and watch you trick a poor old lady out of her legacy.
HOPE	Cook made her own decision. I've forced no one's hand.
MABEL	No? What about cheating Anne and Ted out of *their* share? Yes, I *was* listening behind the curtains! "Three down and four to go", you said.
HOPE	(*swings round*) Keep quiet!
MABEL	Oogh, I got a real earful, I did!
HOPE	(*she moves towards* MABEL) Silence!
MABEL	You're a swindler and murd'ress.
HOPE	Silence! (*Viciously,* HOPE *pushes* MABEL *backwards on to the sofa. She raises her arm to strike . . .*)

AGNES   (*shouts*) Stop it!

          (HOPE *releases* MABEL. *She strides below the armchair and picks up her shawl.* MABEL *sobs bitterly.* AGNES *moves round and comforts her.*)

AGNES   There, there, love. You're all right.

HOPE   I'll deal with her. As for you, Cook — goodbye. You've resigned.

AGNES   Have I 'eck! I'm joining the strike! (AGNES *sits next to* MABEL, *folds her arms, and sets her face bulldoggedly.* HOPE *paces furiously.*)

HOPE   God, what a situation! Surely you realise we cannot go on like this?

MABEL   Why not? Old Mr Barraclough planned it. Rest his soul. So get out your weeji board and tell him!

HOPE   (*still pacing*) Oh, this is futile! (*Cajolingly.*) We've all said things in the heat of the moment. Cook! Carry on with dinner and we shall forget this unfortunate business.

AGNES   No, I'm too het up. I couldn't face that hot stove now.

HOPE   (*shouts*) Damn you! (HOPE *seethes for a second. Then she has a flash of inspriration.*) So I cannot do a thing?

MABEL   That's it, Duchess.

HOPE   Very well. Then by all means lounge around my home, but we shall see how you enjoy watching Anne Beale doing the cooking and the scrubbing for the next six months.

MABEL   (*rises*) You wouldn't dare.

HOPE   Would I not?

MABEL   No — because I'd tell the police everything I heard. Blackmail's a crime, blackmail is.

HOPE   Blackmail? (*She laughs mockingly.*)

AGNES	What's going on, Mabel? (*Rising.*) What is it?
HOPE	(*to* MABEL) Well, make up your mind!
MABEL	The party's over, Aggie. We've got to do as she says.
AGNES	All right, love. Come on, then. (*To* UL.)
MABEL	(*at* HOPE) I don't half hate you! (*Exits.*)
HOPE	Dinner at the usual time, Cook. Not a second later.
AGNES	You've caused a lot of unhappiness, Mum. I reckon you'll be sorry for it. (*Exits.*)
	(HOPE *moves towards the staircase. As she does so, the panel slides open.*)
HOPE	Careful, you fool! (*She enters the recess. The panel slides closed behind her.*)
	(MICKLEBY *hurries down the stairs, followed by* BLUNDELL.)
MICKLEBY	. . . Ghastly, Uncle . . . vanished . . . my heart's bouncing off my eye teeth . . .
	(MICKLEBY, *panting for breath, lies full-length on the sofa.* BLUNDELL *moves to the bookcase panel.*)
BLUNDELL	Standing here, eh? Very odd. But not unexpected. Hmmm! Somehow I feel the answer's at our finger-tips, if only we knew.
	(*He twists the miniature this way and that. The panel slides open and he doesn't notice.*)
BLUNDELL	This picture hook is loose. I wonder if I turned it this way.
	(*He twists it and the panel closes!* BLUNDELL *looks backwards too late.*)
	No good! (*He moves behind the sofa and looks down at* MICKLEBY.) I hope the Doctor's not down that well with the others!
MICKLEBY	(*rises into a sitting position*) Which well?

BLUNDELL	There's an old Druid's well under this floor!
MICKLEBY	Good Lord, is there? (*He snatches his feet up.*)
BLUNDELL	Yes. And I believe old Barraclough and his daughter have been tipped into it forever!

(*Loud thunder clap.*)

MICKLEBY	(*rising*) You don't mean some old druid's behind all this? (*He crosses to* BLUNDELL.)
BLUNDELL	No! Nikkamoppaloffkis. (*He sits in the armchair.*) Now, Nikkamoppaloffkis, in other words, Nicholas Pope, worms his way into the old boy's confidence. Can't you just see Barraclough telling his new actor friend all about his clever secret panels?
MICKLEBY	(*crouching on his haunches*) Keep going, but make it simple.
BLUNDELL	Right! Pope talks himself into a share of the Will. Nasty bit of warmed-up pudding, he is. So he sneaks down here, creeps in the panels, bides his time, and Crunch!! (BLUNDELL *grips* MICKLEBY'S *throat.*)
MICKLEBY	Aaaagh!
BLUNDELL	Ssssh! (*Whispers.*) And he's been here ever since.
MICKLEBY	O-oh-oh-oh! (*Rises and looks around the walls.*) I need something to steady my nerves . . . like a fast train to Brighton.
	(*As* MICKLEBY *turns upstage to look at the back walls,* BLUNDELL *rises and moves below him to* DL, *in deep thought. As a result, when* MICKLEBY *turns a full circle back to the armchair, he thinks* BLUNDELL *has vanished.*)
MICKLEBY	(*yells*) Uncle! Uncle!!
BLUNDELL	(*quietly*) What?

MICKLEBY   Oh! I thought you'd gone to the Druid. (*He hurries over to* BLUNDELL.)

BLUNDELL   Do shut up! I'm reconstructing the crime.

                (BLUNDELL *paces round below the sofa and back above it.* MICKLEBY *follows him, keeping in step.*)

BLUNDELL   (*claps his hands*) Yes! We can only guess how Mr Barraclough got his envelope, but we know how Miss Faith got hers, don't we, boy?

MICKLEBY   Yes. Which envelope?

BLUNDELL   Brains, boy, brains! (*He strides to the desk.*) Only the family are allowed to use this little chest. So the Killer planted one poisoned envelope . . . and removed the others. Simple.

MICKLEBY   Yes, but Uncle – (BLUNDELL *moves below the armchair.*)

BLUNDELL   Don't argue, Mr Mickleby! Anne Beale replenished that envelope chest this afternoon – yet Miss Faith said there weren't any left.

MICKLEBY   (*following* BLUNDELL) And so did Miss Hope.

BLUNDELL   (*irritably*) I *know* Miss Hope . . . Wow! Where's Mabel?

                (BLUNDELL *pauses and claps a hand to his mouth, then hurrying back to the desk, he violently rings the service bell.*)

MICKLEBY   (*follows him*) What're you doing? And why have you gone pale?

                (*Picking up the envelope,* BLUNDELL *opens it then he snaps closed the lid and replaces the chest on the desk.*)

                [N.B. *This Scene is played at breakneck speed, building to the Curtain.*]

BLUNDELL   Empty. Did Mabel say Miss Hope had
           actually used an envelope?

MICKLEBY   Search me. Why?

BLUNDELL   Because if she did, and I am right, she is
           walking this house with a flapful of poison
           inside her.

MICKLEBY   Good grief, she'll be furious.

BLUNDELL   (*pushing him towards the hall*) Mr Mickleby,
           behind the whats'it in the washroom, you will
           see a saucer. Tell me if it has turned black or
           red. Run!

MICKLEBY   I'm not a toilet attendant.

BLUNDELL   If that saucer has turned black, it means Miss
           Hope has been poisoned. Never mind why!
           If that saucer is black, Dr Brown must
           examine Hope and —— great heavens!
           That is why the Doctor was snaffled. (*He
           rushes* MICKLEBY *into the hall.*)

MICKLEBY   Yes but-but-but . . .

BLUNDELL   Run, run, run!

           (MICKLEBY *rushes out.* MABEL *rushes in from the
           kitchen.*)

BLUNDELL   Ah, Mabel! Did Miss Hope actually *use* an
           envelope this afternoon?

MABEL   Yes. She said she'd used the last one.

BLUNDELL   Go find her! Run! Tell her she's been
           poisoned.

MABEL   (*screeches*) Eh?

BLUNDELL   *Run*, child, *run!*

           (*He hurries* MABEL *up the stairs. Then he returns
           to the sofa, exhausted.*)

           (*Shouting after* MABEL.) Try and find the
           Doctor, as well. If he *is* well.

(*With a sigh,* BLUNDELL *lies full-length on the sofa. But* SORRELL *has entered* C. *He moves down swiftly . . . and measures* BLUNDELL *with his tape measure.* BLUNDELL *leaps up with a yelp.*)

BLUNDELL   Mr Sorrell, do you know anything about medicine?

SORRELL   No-ogh. Don't believe in it.

BLUNDELL   Oh dear. I mean poisons and their treatment. In your profession you must often chat with doctors.

SORRELL   No-ogh. When I arrive the doctor's lost interest.

BLUNDELL   Oh never mind.

(SORRELL *sits on the sofa.*)

BLUNDELL   (*surmising to himself*) Let's say Faith wrote her letter at fifteen minutes to three, and we read the Will at twenty past . . . Mmmm. It took roughly half an hour to act.

SORRELL   (*quickly*) Too late, it's too late.

BLUNDELL   How do you know?

SORRELL   (*darkly*) It's always too late.

BLUNDELL   (*consults his watch*) Quarter to five! Say fifteen minutes since Hope licked her envelope. No, there's still time!

MICKLEBY   (*skidding in from the hall*) Uncle, that saucer's gone black.

BLUNDELL   Dead black?

MICKLEBY   Black as death.

SORRELL   (*makes note in little book*) Saucer in Washroom.

BLUNDELL   (*pushing* MICKLEBY) Rush to the Cook! Bring some . . . I don't know . . . bring some milk. Lots of milk . . . anything!

MICKLEBY   Right! (*He rushes out into the kitchen.*)

BLUNDELL	(*to* SORRELL) Miss Hope's been poisoned. (*Dashing upstairs.*) Find the Doctor. You won't — but try! (*He exits.*)

(SORRELL *calmly looks at his watch, then rises. He moves towards the study.*)

SORRELL   Nothing but turmoil, boom and clatter. That's why I like lilies. (*He takes one from the table.*) They never make a noise. (*He shakes the lily ... just as the great bell clangs.* SORRELL *exits, listening in wonderment.*)

(*And now the panel slide open and* HOPE *emerges. The panel closes, and she stands a moment, swaying slightly and grasping the hallway pillar for support. Tightly grasping her shawl about her, she moves weakly to the armchair and sits.*)

MABEL   (*hurrying down the stairs*) Oh, there you are, Miss! (*Goes to her.*) Is it true, Miss? What he said?

HOPE   What *are* you babbling about, Girl?

MABEL   Mr Blundell said you'd been poisoned.

HOPE   Poisoned? (*Clutches her throat.*) *Poisoned*, did you say?

MABEL   Oh yes'm. Envelopes or something. And I can't find the Doctor, Miss. Oh dear. Can't find him.

HOPE   Forget the Doctor. Come here!

MABEL   Oh my gawd. What will you do?

HOPE   Listen to me! (*Fiercely, she grabs* MABEL'S *arm.*)

You're to go to my room. In the top drawer of my bedside table —.

MABEL   Hadn't I better fetch Mr Blundell?

HOPE   (*hissing*) *Listen calmly!* There's a small bottle.
                An antidote. A cure for this poison. Bring it!
                (*She thrusts* MABEL *away and clutches the edges of
                her shawl.*)

MABEL   Oh gawd.

HOPE   Bring the bottle! Bring it! Now!

MABEL   Yes, Miss. Don't you worry, Miss. (*Hurrying
                up the stairs.*) I'll get it. Don't worry. (*Exits.*)

                (HOPE *is breathing heavily, eyes narrowed in
                frightened, furious thought. She heaves herself from
                the chair and moves behind it. The panel opens.*)

HOPE   The envelopes! Caught in my own ... my
                own trap!

                (*A Shrouded Figure is vaguely discernable in the
                recess. Its arm appears holding a knife.* HOPE *is
                unaware. She grows weaker, leaning against the
                chair back for support and, with both hands,
                grasping the shawl tightly to her throat. She hisses
                breathlessly to herself.*)

HOPE   But I prepared for it, Partner! And now
                you've ... you've signed ... you've signed
                your own ... death warrant.

                (*The knife is thrown!* HOPE *jerks her head
                backwards. With a throaty gasp, she twists full
                circle. We see the knife buried in her back.
                Trembling, she sinks to the floor. The panel closes.*)

                [NB: *The knife is thrown on "death" and* HOPE
                jerks her shawl on the word "warrant".]

MABEL   (*returning down the stairs*) I've got the bottle.
                I've got it, Miss. I've got your ... ...

                (*Seeing the prostrate* HOPE, MABEL *stops halfway
                down the stairs and screams shrilly.*)

                CURTAIN

MUSIC

ACT TWO
Scene Three

Midnight.

When the curtain rises a violent struggle is being enacted between two figures in the darkness. Thuds, yelps, grunts. Finally there is one crash louder than the rest.

MICKLEBY   Got you! Thought you could snuff me out, eh! Well hard luck! Now let's have a look at you.

             (*The lights come on.* MICKLEBY *is standing by the switch. There are cushions strewn about. The sofa is upturned, its seat facing upstage.*)

             (*In awe and fear.*) Good Lord – You!

             (*From behind the sofa,* BLUNDELL *rises. His head is protruding through the "Laughing Cavalier" painting from the hall.*)

BLUNDELL   As ever was. Get this art gallery from my neck!

MICKLEBY   Yes, sir. At once Mr Blundell-sir.

             (MICKLEBY *pulls off the painting – almost bringing his Uncle's head with it. Then he hurries it back to the hall, and returns.* BLUNDELL *has clambered over the sofa to sit on its upturned edge.*)

MICKLEBY   You see, sir, I thought you were the Killer returning to the scene of your crime.

BLUNDELL   Couldn't you've said "Who Goes There!" or something?

MICKLEBY   My motto's "Shoot First And Ask Who Went There!". .... (*Brushing* BLUNDELL's *jacket.*) Hope you're not annoyed, Sir.

BLUNDELL   (*smiling beautifully*) Annoyed? As if I should be ... you've only broken my neck ... You Blithering Ape! It's midnight. Why were you down here, anyway?

MICKLEBY   Because I woke up and found *you'd* gone. (*He sits beside* BLUNDELL *on the upturned sofa.*) I wasn't stopping in the late Mr Barraclough's bed all by myself.

BLUNDELL   It didn't stop you sleeping.

MICKLEBY   Ooogh! – ten minutes, that's all I had. And I spent that with a nightmare. (*Massaging his toe.*) I dreamt I was drinking tea with those three dead bodies and that guinea pig. The guinea pig was being 'mother'. It kept winking at me, saying 'Guess who's next!' . . . Why're you down here?

BLUNDELL   I came to consult a medical book in the library.

             (*A loud groan emanates from the chest.*)

CHEST   Oh-oh-oh-oh-ooogh.

             (BLUNDELL *and* MICKLEBY *immediately spring up.* MICKLEBY *grabs his Uncle's hand. They stand rigidly side-by-side.*)

MICKLEBY   Uncle, th-there's s-s-something in agony in the old o-o-oak ch-ch-chest.

CHEST   Oh-oh-oh-oh-ooooogh.

BLUNDELL   Go and see who it is!

             (*He pushes* MICKLEBY *forward, then hides behind the sofa.* MICKLEBY *takes a couple of steps, then turns.*)

MICKLEBY   Uncle! UNCLE!!

BLUNDELL   (*head pops up*) Sssssh!

MICKLEBY   (*indignantly*) Ooogh!

BLUNDELL   Go on! It's your turn. (*Pops down again.*)

             (*Reluctantly,* MICKLEBY *gingerly lifts the lid of the old oak chest. A hand protrudes for a second, then slides back.*

MICKLEBY *drops the lid with a yowl and stands frozen to the spot, staring ahead, hands and arms, and body, stiff with fright. He stands several seconds — then* BLUNDELL'S *head pops up — puzzled.* BLUNDELL *rises and moves round to look at his nephew ... bending his arms with great effort. But* MICKLEBY *remains stiff.*)

BLUNDELL Darwin was right! (*Yells in* MICKLEBY'S *ear.*) Income Tax!

(*This at last brings* MICKLEBY *to life.* BLUNDELL *pushes him aside and (with a look at heaven) bravely opens the lid.*)

It's the Doctor!

MICKLEBY Is he dead?

BLUNDELL Yes — that's why he's groaning. Give me a hand.

(*They help* DR BROWN *from the chest.* MICKLEBY *removes a gag from the* DOCTOR'S *mouth.*)

DOCTOR Thenk you, Gentlemen, thenk you!

BLUNDELL All right, are you, sir?

DOCTOR Somebody chloroformed me. Fine now ... little dizzy ... soon wear off.

BLUNDELL Any idea who did this, Doctor?

DOCTOR I am not knowing anything. They come alongside behind me a few minutes ago and everything is going black.

MICKLEBY Longer than a few minutes, Doc! You've been missing eight hours.

DOCTOR Good gracious, there is a thing!

BLUNDELL Yes, there *are* a thing! Well! We're still marooned, I fear. So you'll have to bed down in the room we've been allocated.

DOCTOR Ach, most kind. Most kind.

(*The* DOCTOR *crosses* BLUNDELL *and heads for the stairs.*)

BLUNDELL   I'll show you the way, sir.

DOCTOR   No no! I know the way. Don't fuss! (*He trips on the bottom step and flounders.* BLUNDELL *helps the* DOCTOR *to his feet.*) Ah, thenk you. These spectacles are shocking.

BLUNDELL   Oh, one moment, sir! (BLUNDELL *moves up and meets the* DOCTOR *half up the stairs.*)

DOCTOR   Did somebody speak?

BLUNDELL   What poison would give the appearance of heart failure, Doctor? Need about half an hour to take effect?

DOCTOR   Mmm, of course, I do not examine Miss Hope. But possible an arsenic preparation or phosphorous.

BLUNDELL   Thank you, sir. It's something to work on.

DOCTOR   No trouble. Good afternoon! (*Exits upstairs.*)

BLUNDELL   Afternoon! – and it's midnight.

            (*Together they put the sofa right way up, and generally tidy the room.*)

            What d'you make of Dr Brown, then?

MICKLEBY   Heck of a long time to be chloroformed – eight hours!

BLUNDELL   Steady, Mr Mickleby, steady! You're showing signs of intelligence.

MICKLEBY   (*pleased*) Am I? Thank you, Mr Blundell.

BLUNDELL   Yes, strange do all round. After all, we have only the Doctor's word he was attacked. You didn't actually *see* him kidnapped.

MICKLEBY   I said it was him from the beginning. In fact, I have a theory.

(BLUNDELL *interrupts him with a loud imitation yawn.*)

BLUNDELL I'm tired. Let's turn in. (BLUNDELL *steers* MICKLEBY *towards the stairs.*)

MICKLEBY That came on suddenly.

(BLUNDELL *claps a hand over* MICKLEBY'S *mouth. He makes exaggerated stamping noises with his feet. Bewildered,* MICKLEBY *follows suit.*)

BLUNDELL We shall need more blankets if the Doctor's sharing our room. (*He switches out the lights.*)

(*After a second, the study door creaks open. A Figure appears, a torch in its hand. The Figure enters the room, then the torch beam circles the faces of* BLUNDELL *and his Nephew.* BLUNDELL *is grinning broadly.* MICKLEBY'S *face, still behind* BLUNDELL'S *hand, is astounded.* BLUNDELL *switches on the lights.*)

BLUNDELL Hello, Johnson!

JOHNSON (*blinks in the sudden glare*) A neat trick. I fell for it nicely.

MICKLEBY So did I!

BLUNDELL Sorry. But you must beware of creaking boards in old houses.

JOHNSON Sharp ears! I suppose you're wondering what I was doing?

BLUNDELL It *is* a gruesome visit for midnight – Miss Hope's body lying in there … if it still is!

JOHNSON It's there. Nobody thought to close her eyes. The torch kept shining in them.

MICKLEBY Oh-oh-ogh! (*Shivers.*) Can't we talk of bees and flowers?

JOHNSON As a matter of fact …

BLUNDELL You were looking for a certain Confession?

JOHNSON	Anne never told you!
BLUNDELL	No, Mabel did. She was, ah, listening this afternoon.
JOHNSON	(*grim smile*) Trust Mabel.
MICKLEBY	Did you find it?
JOHNSON	No.
BLUNDELL	Didn't find the knife, either, did you!
	(BLUNDELL *produces the knife, wrapped in a cloth, from his pocket. He lays it carefully on the table next to the armchair.*)
JOHNSON	(*belligerently*) Trying to say it's mine, are you!
BLUNDELL	I don't know whose it is, dear boy. Now, why don't you turn in and let *us* find that Confession.
JOHNSON	You?
BLUNDELL	Yes, I think we could *now*. All right?
JOHNSON	I don't understand ... But ok. I hope you know what you're doing.
	(JOHNSON *turns and moves towards the kitchen door.* MICKLEBY *hastily rises and hurries to his Uncle, as* JOHNSON *moves behind him.* JOHNSON *exits.*)
BLUNDELL	The more I think of it, the more I believe the Doctor *was* attacked. (*He closes the lid of the great oak chest.*)
MICKLEBY	Then why so chummy with Johnson? Maybe *he* put the Doc in the old oak chest. He was looking for this knife in the study to wipe the fingerprints off.
BLUNDELL	Hang on! You've given me an idea. If there are fingerprints on that knife, they belong to Dr Brown.
MICKLEBY	You've just said he was innocent.

BLUNDELL   He is.

MICKLEBY   Oooogh (*He flops into the armchair.*)

BLUNDELL   Listen! Our killer is far too clever to leave
           his ... *or her* prints on that knife. So he
           captures Dr Brown ... chloroforms him,
           presses the Doc's fingers on the hilt, stabs his
           accomplice wearing gloves, and returns the
           Doctor unharmed to take the blame!

MICKLEBY   Just a ... just a sec! How d'you know Hope
           was the killer's accomplice?

BLUNDELL   (*smugly*) Because she kept this bottle of the
           correct antidote handy. (*Produces it.*) Why?
           Because she knew the type of poison. How?
           Because she was in league with the killer.
           Simple.

MICKLEBY   (*darkly*) There's an old Mickleby proverb:
           "Smug man so busy looking bull in face – he
           step on cow-slip". (*He raises his shoe pointedly.*
           BLUNDELL *laughs.*)

BLUNDELL   Very good. And since you're so witty, you
           shall find the secret panel *and the killer.*

MICKLEBY   (*rises*) I thought you'd shove my canoe up the
           creek!

BLUNDELL   Are you ready?

MICKLEBY   What for?

BLUNDELL   Splendid! (*Shouts.*) Wakey! Wakey!
           Downstairs Everyone!

           (*Moving below the sofa,* BLUNDELL *shouts
           everywhere – through the doorway* L, *round into
           the hallway, and up the stairs.* MICKLEBY *follows,
           astonished.*)

           Wakey, wakey, ladies and gentlemen! In the
           lounge, please. Everyone in the lounge.

MICKLEBY   (*patting his Uncle's arm*) There, there. Take it easy, Uncle. I'll bring you a glass of milk and a yo-yo to play with.

BLUNDELL   (*grips* MICKLEBY'S *shoulders dramatically*) When they come down, I'm going to say you know the killer's name. Do you understand?

MICKLEBY   (*bewildered, shaking his head*) Yes.

BLUNDELL   But you must pretend you're keeping this name a secret. (*Urgently.*) So in heaven's name *do not tell them*!

MICKLEBY   (*squeaks*) How could I? I don't know.

BLUNDELL   Excellent.

MICKLEBY   Do you know the killer?

BLUNDELL   But of course.

MICKLEBY   Then tell me!

BLUNDELL   Think, Mickleby. Someone you have met since we came to this house.

MICKLEBY   Uncle, you're driving me up the wall.

BLUNDELL   Ssssssh.

     (*Voices off. The landing lights come on.* BLUNDELL *pushes* MICKLEBY UR, *then awaits as* MABEL *appears on the stairs in curlers and lurid negligee.* SORRELL *follows in top hat, black scarf and borrowed nightgown. Then the* DOCTOR *swathed in a rug. Lastly,* AGNES *in homely dressing gown with cream on her face.*)

MABEL   Has something else horrible happened?

BLUNDELL   Sorry to disturb you, gentlefolk.

MABEL   I haven't slept a wink.

SORRELL   I have.

     (ANNE *and* TED *enter from the kitchen, fully dressed.*)

BLUNDELL	Ah, all present. (*Dramatically.*) I called you down, ladies and gentlemen to gaze upon a heel, a rat of the lowest sewer . . . Mr Mickleby.
MICKLEBY	Steady on!
BLUNDELL	This fellow – correction, this warped creature-I-once-called-Hubert, knows the name of the killer. But he refuses to tell me. Don't you!
MICKLEBY	Er . . .

(BLUNDELL *digs him in the ribs.*)

MICKLEBY	(*shouts*) Yes!
ALL	Why? Why? . . . . Etc.
BLUNDELL	I'll tell you why! Because he wishes to feed his vanity. To play the big detective when the Police arrive. Don't you!
BLUNDELL MICKLEBY	} (*together*) Yes!!
BLUNDELL	Ladies and gentlemen, whilst that mad slayer is free to stalk this house, free to wreak his terrible will, each and every one of us is in deadly peril.
JOHNSON	Give me ten seconds. I'll make him talk.

(JOHNSON *strides over, grabs* MICKLEBY *by the throat and, seemingly, lifts him into the air and bounces him up and down behind the armchair.*)

MICKLEBY	Aaaagh! Help!
BLUNDELL	Steady on the throttle, Johnson!

(JOHNSON *stops.* MICKLEBY *has now disappeared behind the armchair.*)

JOHNSON	(*to* BLUNDELL) I'm sorry, sir. I . . . sorry.
BLUNDELL	Quite all right. He didn't hurt you, I trust?

(JOHNSON *returns to* ANNE. MICKLEBY *staggers into view over the chair back. He points balefully towards* JOHNSON.)

MICKLEBY   Oogh, you ... you ... !

(MICKLEBY *notices that his bandage is on the wrong finger. He swops it back to his left.*)

BLUNDELL   Ladies and gentlemen, let us retire. Leave the sinking rat on his own. (*He bears down on* MICKLEBY.) With nought but the howling wind for a friend, he'll be begging to tell us the name. Unless the killer gets him first.

MICKLEBY   Uncle!

BLUNDELL   Away we go! Leave him to it! Goodnight. Goodnight.

(*The employees exeunt up the stairs.* BLUNDELL *ushers out* ANNE *and* JOHNSON L, *then returns to the hallway, and draws the curtains.*)

BLUNDELL   Goodnight – *Rat.*

(BLUNDELL *disappears behind the curtains leaving* MICKLEBY *a pathetic figure, very sorry for himself. After a second, he returns quietly and slaps the ususpecting* MICKLEBY *on the back.*)

MICKLEBY   Aggh!

BLUNDELL   Well done. Magnificent acting.

MICKLEBY   I wasn't too keen on the character you gave me.

BLUNDELL   Oh come, come. You know I only meant half of it.

(BLUNDELL *closes the study door. He does so carefully, fussily, and backs away from it as though measuring and considering.*)

MICKLEBY   Why're you doing a production number on the door?

BLUNDELL	I am pondering on how the killer will come in.
MICKLEBY	Why should he come in here?
BLUNDELL	To kill you. Now I'm going out . . . (*Crossing towards kitchen.*)
MICKLEBY	(*runs after him*) TO KILL ME?
BLUNDELL	Naturally. You are the decoy.
MICKLEBY	Me? A sitting duck? A dead sitting duck?
BLUNDELL	My dear Mickleby, you'll go down in criminal history.
MICKLEBY	Yes. But will I come up again?
BLUNDELL	Sssh. (*Turns out the wall bracket light.*) Tell yourself you're not afraid.
MICKLEBY	What if I don't believe myself?
BLUNDELL	Courage! I shall be watching, guarding. (*Exits.*)
MICKLEBY	I'm not afraid. I'm not afraid. . . .

(MICKLEBY *circles the room. He hurries past the hallway opening. "I'm not afraid", he says, and hurries past the study door. He begins hurrying past everything, until he is running in a fearful circle all around the stage. He stops, panting. The* *Dog howls.*)

I'm not afraid —— I'm petrified.

(MICKLEBY *takes a quick look at the bookcase panel, into the hall, and up the stairs. He backs into Caesar's bust, tentatively feels its cold face over his shoulder, reacts, then smacks its head in revenge. He hurries to the study doorway, then backs on to the dagger point – on the table. Now, he tries bravery, clenching his fists, and swinging round and round defiantly. He grows confident, and sings a little song.*)

(Quaveringly.) Your tiny hand is frozen. Your
tiny hand is froze. Oh yes it's froze . . .

*(The panel slides open. The Hooded Figure
appears and stretches out its hand.* MICKLEBY
*backs towards its clutches, singing. Lightning. A
thunder clap startles him forwards. The panel
closes.)*

*(*MICKLEBY *regains confidence. His singing grows
louder. He even does a little dance, backing to the
bookcase. As he sustains a high note . . . the panel
opens. Again the Hooded Figure reaches out its
hand.* MICKLEBY *backs into the recess, and takes
the hand unthinkingly, does a double-take,
screeches, and is dragged into the recess. The panel
closes. It re-opens seconds later to reveal*
MICKLEBY *still struggling valiantly with the
Hooded Figure.)*

MICKLEBY   Uncle . . . Uncle!

BLUNDELL   *(dashing in)* Hold on, Mickleby! Uncle is here.

(The panel is relentlessly closing. BLUNDELL
manages to grab MICKLEBY'S *hand before it
disappears forever. He edges himself into the recess,
drags* MICKLEBY *to safety but gets his backside
trapped in the closed panel.* MICKLEBY *staggers, a
wet rag. He switches on the wall brackets.)*

Mickleby! I'm trapped, boy, trapped.

*(*BLUNDELL *gesticulates towards the Miniature.
Audience reactions and laughter during this Scene
drown dialogue but* MICKLEBY *gets the message.
He staggers to the Miniature and twists it. The
panel slides open.)*

Good work, Mr Mickleby. Shame you didn't
grab him, though. *(Exits into the recess.)*

MICKLEBY   Grab him? I shall never forgive you for this,
Mr Blundell.

BLUNDELL   Aha! (*He reappears with documents and the revolver.*)

MICKLEBY   Found a gun in there?

BLUNDELL   And Miss Beale's Confession. (*Pockets the envelope.*) Envelope can go for analysis. 'Rather think this may interest you more.

(*Handing* MICKLEBY *the other document, he puts the pistol on the table.*)

MICKLEBY   The missing Will! Some rotten b ... beast must've swapped it when we first arrived. The missing Will, ha! Are you going down that hole to catch the killer?

BLUNDELL   Can't. There's a trap door and it's locked.

MICKLEBY   Don't tell me I've suffered for nothing!

BLUNDELL   On the contrary, Mr Mickleby. I have all the proof I require. The Case is closed! (*Shouts.*) Downstairs again, Everyone! Wakey wakey! (*He opens the hall curtains and calls up the stairs "Wakey-Wakey!"*)

MICKLEBY   (*moving to him*) Oh not again! (MICKLEBY *closes the panel.*)

BLUNDELL   Yes! I am going to announce the villain's name (*Calls* L.) In the lounge, everyone.

MICKLEBY   Is the villain one of the people upstairs?

BLUNDELL   Aha! Wait and see!

MICKLEBY   Mr Blundell, you do realise I almost lost my life just now?

BLUNDELL   Of course I do – and it was a very decent gesture.

MICKLEBY   (*frantic*) Decent? It was bloody heroic! The least you could do is give me a clue.

BLUNDELL   By all means, I shall indeed.

MICKLEBY   (*eagerly*) Yes?

BLUNDELL   "I pitied myself because I had no shoes, till I
               met a man with no feet."

               (MICKLEBY *tackles this riddle with a cunning
               smirk – which becomes utter bewilderment, then
               pity, and finally disgust.*)

MICKLEBY   Oh, play by yourself! (*Moving away.*)

               (*Voices off.* BLUNDELL *backs to the hallway
               curtains, ushering everybody in as they appear on
               the stairs.* ANNE *and* TED *return from the
               kitchen.*)

AGNES   (*still in face cream*) If this keeps up, I'll look
               ghastly in 'morning.

MABEL   Here we go again. (*Donning her negligee over a
               lurid nightie.*)

               (AGNES *sits* L *end on the sofa,* MABLE R *end.*
               ANNE *sits* U/S C *edge of the sofa, and* TED *stands
               beside her.*)

DOCTOR   So you are having found the culprit, young
               man?

BLUNDELL   All in good time, Doctor.

               (DR BROWN *is about to sit in the armchair, but
               very obviously* BLUNDELL *steers him to the desk
               chair.* SORRELL *is last to appear. Equally
               obviously,* BLUNDELL *helps him into the armchair.*)

ANNE   Has your colleague revealed this villain's
               name, then?

BLUNDELL   He didn't know the name, Miss. That was ah,
               a subterfuge to force the killer's hand. An
               attempt has been made on Mr Mickleby's life.

               (*General consternation.*)

MICKLEBY   M'yes. A touch hairy for a while, but I settled
               his hash. Ha ha.

JOHNSON   He got away though, didn't he?

DOCTOR   Speak up! Speak up!

SORRELL	And I doubt you saw who he was, did you?
BLUNDELL	Regrettably no but we did discover one thing of interest. Mr Mickleby, would you kindly demonstrate?
MICKLEBY	Certainly Mr Blundell. Open Sesame ... !

(*He turns the Minature, and the panel opens. They all express astonishment.* MICKLEBY *moves round to stand at the extreme* L. *of the sofa.*)

BLUNDELL	And now I must tell you, ladies and gentlemen, that Miss Hope ...
MABEL	Was the killer's accomplice. (*Apologetically.*) I just happened to overhear, sir. Sorry.
BLUNDELL	No problem, ha ha. Now I determined this fact ah, rather astutely, because Miss Hope ...
MABEL	(*to* AGNES) Knew what the antidote was.
BLUNDELL	M'yes. Now the poison was administered ...
MABEL	Oogh yes, on the ...

(BLUNDELL *claps a hand round* MABEL'S *mouth, but as he removes his hand, she continues.*)

Envelope.

BLUNDELL	(*disgruntled*) We have been a busy little girl, haven't we.
AGNES	How could you see the envelopes were poisoned?
BLUNDELL	(*pleasantly*) Mabel?
MABEL	Yes, I couldn't hear that bit.
BLUNDELL	Well now, ha ha ...
MICKLEBY	Chemical reaction. We soaked the envelope in domestic cleaner. We got the idea from a book-oh, sorry Mr Blundell.

JOHNSON	Look, that killer's escaping. Why don't we follow down that passage?
BLUNDELL	We can't. There is a trap door and it's locked.
JOHNSON	We could break it open. Chase him out! He can't cross that flooded river.
BLUNDELL	But he isn't trying to escape, Johnson! (*Rising.*) For one thing he considers himself perfectly safe. (BLUNDELL *climbs the stairs to a commanding position, and surveys them all over the banisters.*) And for another, 'that killer' is one of the people *in this room.*
	(*An uproar follows with everyone jabbering their denials.*)
BLUNDELL	Please! Please! I can prove this!
AGNES	I hope so, love, or you'll look a bit silly.
BLUNDELL	The culprit, Miss Agnes, is one of the persons mentioned in the Will.
ANNE	All those mentioned are not present, Mr Blundell.
MABEL	No! What about Nicholas Pope. (*She looks meaningly at* SORRELL.)
SORRELL	(*hastily*) It's none of my business, but that envelope scheme seems well within the scope of a doctor. (*He looks meaningly at* DR BROWN.)
DOCTOR	Eh? Who is saying what?
BLUNDELL	Dr Brown was himself attacked. I know he is innocent.
MICKLEBY	(*crossing below stairs*) Surely, Mr Blundell, we are not accusing the ladies!
BLUNDELL	Perspicacity, Hubert, perspicacity.
MICKLEBY	Good Lord, don't say he did it!
BLUNDELL	Who?
MICKLEBY	Percy ... oh never mind.

ANNE   Ted has been with me. He couldn't have attacked Mr Mickleby.

BLUNDELL   (*enjoying himself*) He didn't Miss Beale. Nor is it a lady killer.

MICKLEBY   Yes, but if it isn't . . . and it isn't . . . . (MICKLEBY *backs hurriedly from* SORRELL. *All eyes turn on the Undertaker.* SORRELL *bursts into a long peal of laughter.* BLUNDELL *moves downstairs and whispers to* JOHNSON *who goes to the kitchen door. The ladies all rise and move close to the panel.*)

SORRELL   (*morosely again*) I haven't laughed like that since I laid out the wife's mother.

DOCTOR   (*rising*) But, good gracious, surely Mr Sorrell is not the Killer?

BLUNDELL   No, he isn't (*A pause whilst* BLUNDELL *closes the hall curtains, dramatically.*) . . . . . Mr Nicholas Pope!

    (BLUNDELL *swings round and points at the* DOCTOR, *who makes a dash across* L *running over the sofa. The women scream. The men shout.* SORRELL *backs to the desk.* MICKLEBY *joins* BLUNDELL. JOHNSON *captures* POPE *and forces him into a sitting position on the end of the sofa.*)

MICKLEBY   That's not Nicholas Pope. That's Dr Brown, or I'm Oliver Cromwell.

    (BLUNDELL *purposefully removes the wig from* POPE's *head.*)

BLUNDELL   *Who* are you?

MICKLEBY   Well, cut off my ears and call me Roundhead!

POPE   (*dropping his false accent*) You've made your point. Now would you kindly tell your thug to release me? I can hardly fight you all.

(The Ladies group above the sofa. BLUNDELL *nods to* JOHNSON, *who searches* POPE, *then pulls him to his feet.* JOHNSON *then moves to guard the hall.)*

MABEL It's the actor bloke. He came here once.

POPE *(removes his spectacles)* I'll keep the beard, if you don't mind. I used rather strong glue.

ANNE Is the real Doctor safe?

POPE He's tied up in the old cellars. There's the key to the trap door. *(He throws it at* BLUNDELL.*)*

MICKLEBY Well, you fooled me. Pretty good impersonation!

POPE *(ferociously) Pretty good!* It was brilliant! Faith didn't know it was me she showed into Barraclough's room. I've walked this house many a time and no one suspected.

BLUNDELL Mr Mickleby! *(He takes key to him.)* Pop down and fetch the real Doctor, would you?

MICKLEBY Not too keen on going down there by myself, Uncle.

BLUNDELL I'm sure Mr Sorrell'll keep you company.

SORRELL Why not?

*(*MICKLEBY *turns to face* SORRELL *(just behind him) and is horrified at the prospect.* SORRELL *starts moving quickly –* MICKLEBY *backs before him, in step. They head for the panel.)*

MICKLEBY Oh not with him! .... Ooooogh! ....

*(*MICKLEBY *and* SORRELL *disappear into the panel.)*

POPE *(glowers at* BLUNDELL*)* Blast you! How did you find out?

BLUNDELL We disturbed you down here at midnight.

You couldn't get back to the panel in time so
you hid in the chest and bluffed it out.
Correct?

POPE   You're doing the talking.

BLUNDELL   But in the excitement, you forgot to be deaf!
And Dr Brown always muddles his Am's
Are's and Is's — you didn't.

(*During this speech,* POPE *edges nearer to*
BLUNDELL, *nearer to the pistol on the table!*)

Another thing — we offered to show you to
our bedroom and you said you knew where
to go. But as the Doctor had been missing
eight hours, he couldn't possibly know which
room we were in.

POPE   Could've been absent-mindedness.

BLUNDELL   Possibly, but according to a medical
book . . . . . .

(POPE *makes a sudden lunge for the pistol,*
reaching across the armchair. BLUNDELL *gets there*
first!)

BLUNDELL   According to a medical book I consulted
tonight, no doctor'd say arsenic gave the
impression of heart failure.

POPE   You have to be so careful. So damned
careful.

BLUNDELL   Yes . . . and why did you change the Wills?

POPE   (*savagely*) I didn't change them. Hope did.
She tried to cheat me out of my legacy. I
soon stopped her!

(AGNES *screams shrilly.*)

ANNE   What's the matter?

AGNES   I forgot me teeth! (*She hurries upstairs and*
out.)

MICKLEBY   (*entering from the panel*) The Doc's fine! Fine!
              (*He points suddenly at* POPE'S *shoes.*) By George,
              now I get it! He's wearing shoes!

BLUNDELL   Well done, Mr Mickleby. The final proof.

MABEL   How d'you mean?

BLUNDELL   Simple, Mabel. When the real Doctor arrived
              he was wearing slippers. When we chatted
              with Mr Pope at midnight, he was wearing
              shoes!

MICKLEBY   Hard cheese, Pope! Reckon you slipped up
              there!

POPE   I did not. The damn slippers were three sizes
              too small.

BLUNDELL   Take the gun, Johnson! Lock him up for the
              night.

              (JOHNSON *drags* POPE, *who struggles fiercely and
              frantically.*)

POPE   You won't hold me! None of you! You'll not
              keep me.

              (*At the hall opening,* JOHNSON *pauses to allow*
              POPE *the following lines in the clear.*)

              Watch out, Blundell! And as for you,
              Mickleby, when I get free, God help you!

MICKLEBY   Thank you. I'm glad you're religious. (*He
              backs away.*)

              (JOHNSON *drags* POPE *out, struggling and
              shouting afresh.*)

BLUNDELL   I'll see what's happening below. (*He moves to
              the panel.*) Oh, deal with this, Mr Mickleby.
              (*Hands* MICKLEBY *the confession.*) Excuse me,
              Ladies. (*He exits through the panel.*)

MABEL   (*crossing to the stairs*) Oogh, I'll never forget
              this horrific night.

MICKLEBY	(to ANNE) Mr Blundell thinks you should burn this.
ANNE	(takes the confession) Thank you. Thank you very much.
	(She kisses his cheek and exits. Grinning pleasurably, MICKLEBY turns towards MABEL.)
MABEL	Coo! I'll have a bash at that! (MABEL swings him into her arms, and plants a resounding kiss. Then she puts a coin in his hand.) Another shilling for your trouble. Ta ta! (She exits upstairs.)
MICKLEBY	(ecstatically) No doubt about it! I've that little extra zing the girls adore!
	(SORRELL enters from the panel and goes straight upstairs.)
SORRELL	Take it easy there, Doctor. I'm running out of brass handles.
	(Now DR BROWN appears, followed by BLUNDELL. The DOCTOR moves to the stairs.)
DOCTOR	Most puzzlink. Standink here, I is . . . and everythink am going black. I must look at my livers.
	(He trips on the bottom step.)
BLUNDELL	Mr Sorrell, would you help him upstairs?
SORRELL	(nods glumly) Usually help people downstairs.
	(He takes the DOCTOR's hand.)
SORRELL DOCTOR	(as they exit) Good morning. Good afternoon.
BLUNDELL	Good night.
MICKLEBY	Another day gone!

BLUNDELL   (*closing the panel*) Mr Mickleby, the lark's on
            the wing, all's right with the world. (*His smile
            fades when he sees* MICKLEBY'S *worried face.*)
            Cheer up! What's wrong?

MICKLEBY   If Nicholas Pope ever does get free, they'll
            change the name of our Firm.

BLUNDELL   What to?

MICKLEBY   Rigor, Rigor and Mortis.

            (BLUNDELL *laughs, puts his arm around*
            MICKLEBY, *and they exit upstairs.*)

            CURTAIN

KNIFE-THROWING ILLUSION

First bore a hole in the Thrower's knife and attach it to a glove with strong wire. This knife is palmed by the Hooded Figure.

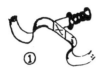

Next construct a dummy knife (preferably from aluminium, but painted wood will serve.) Most of the blade is bent at a right-angle. Bore holes in this angled part and sew it to a thin piece of webbing, or other strong cloth, measuring four feet by two inches.

FIGURE ONE.

When the webbing is worn across the shoulders the weight of the knife will cause it to hang downwards at the back.

FIGURE TWO

A sharp tug on the ends of the webbing will bring the knife upwards to press flush against the nape of the neck . . . thus appearing to be firmly embedded in the luckless victim.

FIGURE THREE

The webbing should now be sewn into the edges of a shawl. This must be done in such a way that the folds of the shawl conceal the knife when the webbing is held loosely.

CUE LINE: (Act Two, Page 86):

The Killer "throws" his knife on the word ". . . death . . ." HOPE tugs the edges of the shawl and jerks forward with a gasp on the word ". . . . war-rant".

If the palming of the knife and HOPE's reactions are perfectly synchronised, this stage effect is most startling. As an added refinement, HOPE may carry a duplicate shawl during the Play . . . which is substituted for the trick shawl just prior to her final Entrance.

FURNITURE AND PROPERTY PLOT

Carpet on floor. Writing table DR with desk chair or stool. Small brass bell, old tea chest or box for envelopes, pen and ink set, blotter etc, a lamp for dressing, and old fashioned telephone. Bell rope on wall by desk. Armchair RC and small drum table. Occasional table below stairs UR, on it a bowl of lilies. Caesar's bust on pedestal. Small chair UL by Sliding Panel. Miniature painting (to open panel). Sofa LC with single end and no back. Heavy oak chest (to accommodate Dr Brown). Heavy damask curtains to draw across hallway C. "Laughing Cavalier" or other appropriate painting, and duplicate with centre hole cut. Atmospheric dressing: books for wall-case DL, a suit of armour (if available), paintings, miniatures, antique pistols and wall lighting brackets.

Thunder sheet, rain/wind effect; dog howls, owl hoots.

ACT ONE   Scene One

Set:	Table L of armchair
	Chair in front of Panel UL
	Black gloves Upstairs
	One letter on desk
	One envelope in desk box
	Revolver in desk drawer
	Dummy arm OFF R
	2 overcoats Hallway R
	Cup of tea OFF L (Anne)
	2 cups of tea OFF L (Mabel)
	Glass of brandy OFF L
	Envelopes OFF R
	Powder in suit of armour
FAITH:	Veil
MICKLEBY:	bowler hat
BLUNDELL:	bowler, briefcase & Will
DOCTOR:	bag, stethoscope
KILLER:	black drape with eye slits

Scene Two

Remove:	Chair from in front of Panel
	Bowlers from table UR
	Envelopes from box
Set:	Table R of armchair
	Broken telephone cord
	One envelope in box
	Loose lilly in bowl UR
	Plate of Sandwiches OFF L
HOPE:	Veil, handkerchief
MABEL:	Apron, shilling
SORRELL:	2 brochures, little book and pencil, tape measure

ACT TWO   Scene One

Remove:	Sandwiches from beneath sofa
Set:	Table to L of armchair
	Lily (from oak chest) into bowl UR
	Torch in Study OFF R (Blundell)
BLUNDELL:	Watch, duplicate antidote bottle for Scene Two.
MICKLEBY:	Finger bandage
JOHNSON:	Revolver
HOPE:	Folded letter in dress
MABEL:	Handkerchief, letter

Scene Two

Check:	Confession and Will behind Panel
	Revolver behind Panel
	Trick shawl in working order
	Loose lily UR for Sorrell
Set:	Antidote bottle Upstairs
	Killer's glove with knife attached behind Panel.
MABEL:	Cocktail glass, shilling
HOPE:	Trick shawl

Scene Three

Remove:	"Laughing Cavalier" painting
Set:	Sofa overturned, cushions scattered
	Duplicate painting by sofa (Blundell)
DOCTOR:	Gag; cellar key
JOHNSON:	Torch
MABEL:	Shilling

*** **** ***

LIGHTING PLOT

Sources of light: 3 wall brackets, and from Hallway C, and window DR. The walls should be kept as dark as possible to enhance the mystery aspect, and the main acting areas kept bright to assist the comedy. There are five main acting areas: stage C, and around the armchair, around the sofa, on the stairs, and the sliding panel.

Exterior floods: Green in Study, Amber from Upstairs, Red shining from doorway L, Blue through the window DR, and a White Flood in these positions for lightning effect. Lightning floods are flashed before each thunder clap.

ACT ONE

Scene One

Open with all exteriors On. One spot on the armchair; one Green Spot on the hallway opening (which can remain on throughout the play). All other sources Off.

Cue 1:	Snap up to Full (including wall brackets).
Cue 2:	Fade everything to a 1/4 except the Green Spot on the Hallway.

Scene Two

Full lighting, but kill exterior window Flood.
Change Hallway flood to Green.
No Cues.

ACT TWO

Scene One

The Same. No Cues

Scene Two

The Same. No Cues.

Scene Three

Open on D.B.O. except for Hallway Green Spot.

Cue 1:	Snap on full lighting except for Upstairs Flood.
Cue 2:	Snap off to D.B.O. except for Green Study Flood. After 10 seconds: snap up to Full Lighting.
Cue 3:	Upstairs Flood on Servants entrance.
Cue 4:	Snap off Study Wall Brackets and corrresponding Spots; and dim to 3/4.
Cue 5:	Snap on Study Wall Brackets

STAGE PLAN